HEART & *Craft*

BESTSELLING ROMANCE WRITERS SHARE THEIR SECRETS WITH YOU

Valerie Parv

HEART & *Craft*

BESTSELLING ROMANCE WRITERS SHARE THEIR SECRETS WITH YOU

Valerie Parv

ALLEN&UNWIN

BOR

First published in 2009

Allen & Unwin
83 Alexander Street
Crows Nest NSW 2065
Australia
Phone: (61 2) 8425 0100
Fax: (61 2) 9906 2218
Email: info@allenandunwin.com
Web: www.allenandunwin.com

Cataloguing-in-Publication details are available from the
National Library of Australia
www.librariesaustralia.nla.gov.au

ISBN 978 1 74175 721 7

Text design by Liz Seymour
Typeset in Fairfield LH 11.5/16pt by Midland Typesetters, Australia

Printed in Australia by McPherson's Printing Group

10 9 8 7 6 5 4 3 2 1

CONTENTS

WELCOME
to our world

I don't think anybody can absorb all of craft at
once; you have to learn by doing, and I think
that goes on forever.
—*Jennifer Crusie, Hearts Talk, May 2007, p. 13*

Welcome to the world of romance writing. This book is about learning by doing. More precisely, it is about how the contributors—all multi-published romance writers, many of whose novels regularly feature on international bestseller lists—learned by doing.

Every new writer hears of a gazillion 'rules' to be followed—show, don't tell; use active, not passive voice; start in the middle of the action; write up to the 'black moment' when things can't possibly get any worse for your characters. You end up wondering how you'll ever master all these elements while getting down on screen the story in your head clamouring to be written.

As Jennifer Crusie says, it's impossible to learn all the elements of the writing craft at one go. For most writers, it takes years and many books. Some of us look back on our early published works and shudder, wishing we could bury or burn them, or at least rewrite the more awkward passages. Some bestselling authors go as far as buying back the rights to those first books so they can sink them without a trace. But the truth is, they were good enough to be published. They weren't perfect, and they didn't need to be. They possessed a spark of originality which grabbed the editors' attention, prompting them to buy the books out of the thousands in their teetering slush pile of unsolicited manuscripts. When we submitted our early books, we thought they were the best things we had ever written. And at the time, they were. It's only with hindsight and increasing mastery that we become aware of the flaws we couldn't see back then. We learned by doing, and you can, too.

In the process, we've been asked the same questions many times: Where do you get your ideas? How long does it take you to write a book? Is there a formula for writing romance? How much money can you make? Most of us have a hard time answering the rest—and the last question, of course, is nobody's business but ours. I wrote an entire master's thesis in an attempt to deal with the ideas question. And I love the answer Nora Roberts gave when we did an ABC Radio interview together in Sydney. When asked how long does it take, she said, 'As long as it takes, every time.'

As for the formula, most of us wish there was such a beast. It would be far easier to fill in the gaps in a (mythical) computer template than to challenge ourselves to come up with fresh new stories about living, breathing characters falling in love against the odds in their own unique ways.

The frequency and seriousness with which the questions come up at writers' conferences, during media interviews or in social gatherings, tell me there is really only one thing most people want to know: how do we do what we do? For those of you who wish to write your own books, the rider is: how can you do it too?

There are already many how-to-write books available—including my own, *The Art of Romance Writing* (Allen & Unwin, 2004)—designed to help you improve your knowledge of the writing craft. However, the best way to get down to the nitty-gritty of those nagging questions is to chat one-to-one with successful writers about their creative practices, which can be as different from each other as the proverbial chalk and cheese.

Writers' lives are as hectic as most people's these days, so it's hard to get time to talk about how we write. Mostly we're too busy juggling writing with the demands of families, homes, businesses, pets and plain old everyday life. Even attending writers' conferences is a luxury, with most of us rationing ourselves to one or two every couple of years, when we're likely to be speaking or giving workshops, limiting the chance to mix and mingle even more.

We've come together in this book so you can sit down, figuratively speaking, with some of the most successful romance writers in the business and share experiences. Each contributor agreed to enlarge on two aspects of their writing: the anecdotal (how they came to do what they do) and their tricks of the trade (how you can apply some of their methods to your own work).

Most of the contributors agree that there's no one way to write a romance novel, no 'secret' that can be applied to every writer and every story. The best advice is to try the various methods and see what works for you. If you're a night owl, my preferred method of rising with the sun and working before the rest of the world is awake will seem like torture to you, just as working late into the night does to me.

Then there are the 'pantsers' versus the 'plotters'. Pantsers are called so because, like the old-time pilots, they're said to fly by the seat of their pants, mostly by instinct. Plotters work the opposite way, creating detailed outlines, graphs, charts and character biographies before they start writing. Asking a pantser to write a synopsis before they've written the book is verging on cruelty, although editors generally want to see an outline and sample chapters before commissioning a book. A plotter is more at home in this environment, happy to provide all kinds of sample material to help the editors make up their minds. A fortunate few writers are 'plotsters', producing their books through a combination of planning and serendipity. Trying to switch when one or the other is your natural way of working is like trying to paint new spots on a leopard. The result is seldom pretty. We recommend you stick to what works for you.

It's not necessary to work through this book from beginning to end. Dip in anywhere that takes your fancy, perhaps starting with a chapter by a writer whose work you already love, and settle down for a cosy insight into how they work their word magic.

One of the most popular elements at writers' conferences is the panel discussion, when a number of writers toss ideas back and forth, sometimes agreeing, more often agreeing to disagree. This element has been provided in the form of the chapters on aspects of the writing craft concluding the book. Here you'll find short takes from all of us on everything from how we create our characters, handle viewpoint or write dialogue, to dealing with writing as a career.

Each author has contributed her thoughts on the different themes, from writing the dreaded synopsis, to bringing characters to life. The advice is brief, and occasionally contradictory because of our different approaches. Again, use only what resonates with you.

Finally, it's important to bear in mind that romance writing, like any other form of fiction, is a fluid, ever-changing medium. Just as yesteryear's governesses and secretaries gave way to this century's kick-butt action-adventure heroines, the sexy werewolves and vampires of trendy urban fantasies will inevitably be replaced by some other, as yet undreamed of, phenomenon. Undreamed of until you write them into your romance novel, sending the genre off in yet another new direction. Then you can come and tell us how you did it, for a sequel to this book. In the meantime, enjoy visiting the many worlds of romance writing.

VALERIE PARV

1

CHANGING *with the times*

ROBYN DONALD

First, a confession.

My writing muse and I have a love/hate relationship.

Oh, it wasn't always so; when first I started to write I adored it, and religiously stole time from a busy life to scribble. I bubbled with (mostly) silent excitement whenever I could find the time to sit down with my pen in my hand. In those days I couldn't type, and the only office I had was the dining table, but the thrill of seeing the words that seethed around my brain transmitted onto paper made up for cramping fingers and a sore back.

In those days I knew nothing about the publishing business, nothing about writing a novel. My only source of information was a book called *Teach Yourself to Write*. I studied the grammar section most intently. It's long gone now, and I have no idea who the writer was, but I salute him or her—my first inklings of professionalism came from that book.

But what I did have was a huge enthusiasm for reading romances, and a burning desire to be able to reproduce the intensity of the experience for my own pleasure. I didn't think of actually finishing a manuscript, or sending it away to see if I was any good at what I was doing.

So for the next ten years I wrote by hand on lined college paper. And wrote. And wrote . . .

I had no idea of just how much I didn't know. I didn't plot. I didn't need to worry about finding the perfect final sentence for a book, because I never finished a manuscript. When things got to the point where I had to actually come up with reasons for my characters' actions, I lost interest, ruthlessly abandoned them and started on the next exciting couple who were urging me to tell their story.

This meant that although I had lots of practice in writing the beginnings of books, I had none at all when it came to ending them—something I still have problems with. I wish I'd practised that more.

Without realising what I was doing or attempting to analyse techniques or methods, I tried to reproduce what I loved about the books of my favourite writers, such as Anne Weale, Violet Winspear, Celine Conway and Essie Summers, a grand New Zealand writer. Before I'd ever heard the term I dreamed up alpha heroes and gave them spirited heroines, I wrote—for pages!—of the scenery in my country, and I tried with everything in me to achieve the exciting emotional tension that I enjoyed so much. Character arcs? Never heard of them. Archetypes? Well, I knew about them, but certainly never understood that they had any relevance to what I was doing. I was just having the most enormous fun in what was probably the longest and least useful apprenticeship any writer ever had!

And then my husband suffered a heart attack, and while he was recovering he suggested I finish the book I was working on and send it off. So of course I did. I got a friend to type it, then packaged it up and sent it off to the address at the front of the books I enjoyed the most—those published by Mills & Boon.

Query letter? Synopsis? I'd never heard of either.

Miraculously, my book was accepted with a few revisions—mainly making sure I kept religiously to the heroine's point of view, because that's what readers wanted in those days. Oh, and I had to cut out a couple of sunsets and quite a bit of rather evocative descriptions of scenery that had no action in them, and so weren't telling the reader anything beyond that I liked the New Zealand countryside.

Because of the twelve-hour time difference between the publishing office in London and New Zealand, the acceptance arrived in a letter, which was how all communication was conducted. Even airmail took a week—one way. Everything was done at a distance.

Elated, all my dreams, hopes and yearnings achieved, I wrote another book. It was accepted too. Such excitement! But I kept my day job as a remedial reading teacher. For the next five years I just went on doing what I'd been doing before—although, looking back, I realise now that I was forming ideas of structure, and that I'd always known that a novel went nowhere without conflict. And I continued to read romances—and every other form of literature—voraciously. I even dimly recognised that I had a voice that was unique to me.

BLISSFULLY IGNORANT

Mills & Boon was the perfect publisher for a total amateur. At that time they didn't send out copyedits or galley proofs, which made life very simple. They published the books all over the world and I wasn't expected to help sell them. Blissfully ignorant of such mundane things as publishing schedules and marketing concerns, I went on writing. No one ever mentioned a deadline. If there were bestseller lists, I hadn't heard of them.

(Computers? I think that right then there was only one in the world, and it took up a whole city block somewhere in America.)

After two years of royalty statements, I realised I was earning as much from my writing as I was from teaching. If I gave up teaching—by then a part-time position—I could write more books. So I resigned.

But my book production didn't increase. I treated my writing as an exciting hobby that earned money. It was far too easy to waste time doing the activities I'd neglected for years, and of course there were other distractions— ones I was only too pleased to indulge. Unfortunately, I still believed that real writers waited for inspiration to strike—and I was having too much fun as a stay-at-home person for my muse to get a look-in.

However, I began to be assailed by a feeling I was uncomfortable with—guilt, because I wasn't writing. I tried to ignore it. As a teacher I'd been proud to be professional, but I'd never thought of professionalism in relation to writing. About the only professional advance I made was to learn to touch type—fast, and very badly. Actually, I never thought of writing as a *career*—it was a joy, a wonder, an invitation to my too-vivid imagination to let rip whenever my muse made an appearance. Which she was doing less and less.

Then my editor came to New Zealand for a visit.

I don't think I've ever been as excited as I was at the prospect of this meeting. By the time she arrived

I hadn't slept for two nights. And she, after surviving a trip in a tiny plane and a landing through a hole in the clouds at our tiny country airport, introduced me to a few alien concepts.

One was that publishers actually had some idea of what they wanted their writers to produce. Another was that it was a good thing for writers to produce regularly and as frequently as they could. This, my editor explained, built name recognition. It simply hadn't occurred to me that part of a writer's success in category fiction was providing a regular supply of new books to keep their name before the readers.

SCARY THOUGHTS

Discussing my writing with my editor made me realise that yes, actually, I did have a career. People in that office on the other side of the world were seriously depending on me to write books. It was a scary thought.

However, shortly after that I made the acquaintance of two other romance writers who lived reasonably close to me—both of whom were infinitely more knowledgeable about writing and the romance publishing world than I was. Thank you Helen Bianchin and Daphne Clair. Drawing on their knowledge and experience, I began to learn something about the process of getting a book out to its readers.

To my shock, writing for the sheer joy of it, without thought of selling or even being read by anyone, began to fade once I realised that others were depending on me to produce books—in other words, when what had been shameless self-indulgence turned into my job. This meant I had to work out ways to continue producing without that initial carefree pleasure. Perhaps it's just as well I didn't understand until much later how precarious a writer's career could be. Appreciating just how difficult writing to a deadline often is might well have curbed my spontaneity. I might have been more than a little put off to realise that every writer is only as good as their last sales.

But all these revelations were in the future, and I had other things to think about . . . I had just got my first computer!

At first I considered computers to be nothing more than glorified typewriters, until I was persuaded, by my husband and a charming salesman with a penchant for chocolate fish, to try the very first Macintosh. Love at first sight! However, I was warned by my editor that the London office wasn't computerised, so the manuscripts still went off in the traditional way, although courier services were making the turnaround time a lot faster.

Meanwhile, things were happening elsewhere in the world. In the early eighties readership in North America boomed, and another publisher decided to enter the scene, launching Silhouette Books. The new authors were mainly North American; their fresh voices appealed to me—and to other readers— enormously.

Feminism was on the rise, and when women changed their attitudes men were forced to not only accept that, but to do the same. My heroines and heroes changed accordingly; avenues opened up for heroines, and men—even romantic heroes—had to learn that they could no longer get by on their alpha qualities and a strong protective instinct. They couldn't just bark out orders and expect them to be obeyed. Heroines no longer felt obliged to conform to societal pressures to seem demure and compliant. While they had always been determined to do what they thought was right for them, they now had far more choices and more freedom.

As a writer I wanted to indicate that the balance of power had shifted, while still keeping the tension strong and powerful and the love story as riveting as ever. Because I tend to write instinctively, this proved challenging. Instead of just sitting down and writing without boundaries, I had to think hard about what I was doing.

Complicating this was a discovery: when reading the new North American writers I was intrigued by their depictions of the hero's internal struggle.

TENSIONS AND JOYS

For decades the sole point of view in a romance had been the heroine's, and for a very good reason—writing from a single point of view is a valid and useful way to increase tension to a sometimes almost unbearable level.

As a reader, I relished the tiny, fascinating clues that revealed the hero's building love for the heroine. Seeing his actions from the heroine's point of view only, coloured by her insecurity about this growing attraction, her wonder and confusion about her growing love and the 'does he, doesn't he?' push–pull of emotions, had added enormously to the intensity of my reading experience. As a writer I found this slow, incremental way of building character and tension a joy to create.

> He flashed her another fierce glance, then smiled, reached for her hand, and tucked it beneath his own on the wheel, only releasing it when they reached the small town on the way home. Lexie let it rest in her lap, oddly chilled by the subtle rejection . . . what if he was ashamed of wanting her?
>
> *Innocent Mistress, Royal Wife*

Poor Lexie! I resisted including the hero's point of view for a long time. However, once I took the plunge

I found I enjoyed writing from his angle. When well done, it gives extra depth and texture to a novel.

> The questions Rafiq couldn't ask nagged at him. Had [Lexie] responded to Gastano with the same wildfire passions she'd revealed in his own arms?
>
> The thought made his fist clench. Watching the way the golden lamplight shifted and shimmered across her bent head as she carefully sorted the chessmen, Rafiq wondered again if his objectivity was being hijacked by his response to her.
>
> *Innocent Mistress, Royal Wife*

Of course there's the reverse too; *clumsily* done, using more than one viewpoint can slow the pace unbearably by delivering information the reader has already discerned from the hero's actions and body language, his tone of voice and his conversation.

As well, the advance of technology has made writing more difficult when it comes to plotting. I found the advent of mobile phones particularly irritating; if people could be in constant contact, some of my most cherished plot points failed entirely. Fortunately the network didn't cover every part of New Zealand (it still doesn't) so I could work around that, but it was the change of attitude in the characters that challenged me as a writer.

One thing that hasn't changed is that I'm an organic writer.

TO PLAN OR NOT TO PLAN

Writers are divided into two main groups—those who plan their books and those who don't. I don't. And it's not a matter of choice. I *can't* plan my books. I call myself an organic writer. This means I start each manuscript with a couple of names, a setting, a house, and a dim idea of the conflict—or the 'source of tension', as Daphne Clair and I decided it should be called after reading one too many manuscripts marred by the writer's reliance on misunderstandings and bickering to keep the two main protagonists out of each other's arms.

And I have been known to change everything—especially names—halfway through a book if it's not gelling for me.

Quite frequently I only discover the fundamental source of tension—the back story that has scarred the hero, or the decision made in the heroine's youth which prevents her from trusting any man—when I'm well into the book and know more about my characters. Often that means I have to go back and rewrite large chunks of the preceding manuscript to fit in with this new knowledge.

So for me, each new manuscript involves a huge amount of rewriting because I tend to wander off down interesting byways that eventually turn out to lead nowhere. It's an inefficient way of working, but it's the only way for me, because one of the things that keeps me going is my eagerness to discover what happens next.

Once, early in my career, I did plan a book. I read an article by a writer I respected which implied that sitting down and trusting to the muse was a very slack, unprofessional way to tackle writing; it was easier and far more efficient to plot out a book before you actually started to write it. And to show you how simple it was, this writer outlined the process step by step.

I'm a sucker for lists. This looked not only simple, but fun, so I tried it.

Simple? Ha! Crushed to discover that it was incredibly difficult for me to think up plot points and character arcs, I realised that the only way I got to know my characters was by writing about them. As in writing the actual book . . .

However, I persevered until eventually I had a rough chapter-by-chapter breakdown—only to find that after all the angst and hard work, I couldn't write the wretched book because I already knew what was going to happen. For me, writing according to a plan was like painting by numbers—no freedom and no room for creativity.

To other writers, my way of producing a book sounds like a recipe for disaster. And until I worked out for myself that my muse lives in my keyboard, my lack of system slowed my production enormously. It took me quite a while—a matter of years, in fact—to understand this.

But although I'm a slow learner, once the lesson is learned it sticks. I now know that as a professional writer it's no use waiting for inspiration to strike, for the muse to come visiting. I have to go out and hunt her down.

I also wish I'd found out much earlier in my career that although I don't actually seem to be awake until a couple of hours after I get up and drink coffee, this is my best writing time. When I'm writing a book, I get up at five each morning and write until seven, walk the dog and the husband for an hour, skim-read the newspaper and do the cryptic crossword, then go back and write until midday. Under this regime I can produce twelve pages of rough draft each day.

Very rough draft. Turning it into a publishable manuscript involves using a freelance editor with a picky mind and, on my part, lots of heavy-duty rewriting and editing. So much so that, by the time I finish the manuscript and send it away, I'm so weary of it that I never want to see it again.

Well, not until the six author's copies turn up in the mail!

TRY DIFFERENT METHODS

As a writer, you should certainly try different methods of producing a book. Discard the ones that don't work for you. Don't listen to anyone who says that their method is the only way to write—or even the *best* way to write. If you're convinced you're a planner, sitting down at the keyboard and winging it, as I do, will result in nothing but confusion. Plan away.

However, if you're an organic writer, don't try to force yourself into the straitjacket of a plan—and don't let anyone imply that you should.

And keep trying new things, without being discouraged if they don't work. Making collages of characters and backgrounds works brilliantly for some writers. It doesn't do anything at all for me—although I do have a wall in my chaotic office where I can pin photographs of scenes and people I find appealing. I might look at it constantly as I write—or I might never glance its way during a whole book.

Writing in coffee shops is a technique I wish I could master—it sounds so much fun. Unfortunately, the only time I tried it I found myself watching rather than writing. And eating far too many muffins.

I also play music while I write—Queen's music is a special favourite I like to listen to towards the end of a manuscript, but I enjoy all sorts, and what I play depends entirely on the way I feel. Vivaldi is a composer who always seems to get my creative juices flowing. Some writers burn a CD of music that 'fits' the book they're working on, somehow echoing the theme and the mood, and that becomes the signature music for the book.

Does this emphasis on production banish the joy of writing, the freedom of sitting down at a desk and just losing myself in the characters and their story? Yes—and no. I allow myself free rein in the first draft, and I think for me it's partly why I don't plot—I enjoy the wicked pleasure of letting my fingers fly across the keys without even thinking of editing.

Of course, such lack of restraint can come to a grinding halt, leaving me to suffer through hours when I stare at the screen cudgelling my blank brain into producing something—anything!

Another confession: when things are going badly, I don't like writing. I have been known to scrub the kitchen floor—once I found myself *cleaning the oven*—instead of writing, because I didn't know where the book was going next and I was totally convinced I couldn't come up with something.

I've learned to work through these times by just keeping on writing. Sometimes I'll produce rubbish that has to be dumped when I'm editing the book, before I send it away; more often it's not. The difficulty had been in my mind, or my mood, or sometimes just the fact that I'd had a bad night.

Often the scenes I labour and worry about most, the ones I am convinced are hopeless and awful and sheer dreck, turn out to be fine. In fact, sometimes I can't even remember which pages they were when I do a final reread of the book.

I've also learned to work through the other things that have changed in my career since I started. Then writers were almost anonymous; there was little or no publicity. Now it's a given—especially among e-publishers—that writers do what they can to publicise their own work. Most publishers also have marketing departments that work hard for each author and every book.

But it helps—although nobody I've ever asked has been able to tell me how much—if the writer is keen to do all she can for her work.

Some writers manage a database of readers and send out a newsletter at fairly regular intervals. Once this went by post; now it's mainly—and more cheaply and widely—conducted over the internet, which has become the most popular way to organise publicity. Most writers at least have a home page; many run interesting and easily accessible websites. Blogs are also very popular with authors, writers and publishers, as are social websites such as MySpace and YouTube. All need regular maintenance to stay interesting and accessible.

As well, groups of readers have set up sites where they can conduct stimulating and often controversial correspondence with each other and with authors. Publishers, too, produce websites with interactive bulletin boards that provide an opportunity for authors to blog and readers to respond.

Other popular ways of meeting readers are author signings at bookstores and attending various conferences to speak.

However, although energetic publicity can build a good reader base, it takes time and effort that some writers feel would be better directed to their work. If that is how you feel, be assured it shouldn't affect your sales in the long term. Plenty of excellent reputations have been built on nothing more than excellent books.

Some top writers never do any publicity, never appear in articles, never show their faces. But they do answer fan letters, and if they get so many it's physically impossible to answer them all, they hire someone to do that work. However, so far I've never met a writer who didn't read *all* the letters they get from readers. Fan letters are a joy and a goad; they urge me towards the keyboard when I want to roll over and go back to sleep, they've given me ideas that worked and some that didn't, and they've made me laugh—and occasionally frown. And they are always answered.

Bride at Whangatapu, the first book I ever finished, was published in 1976. Since then I've had seventy-eight books published in Harlequin/Mills & Boon's Modern/Presents/Sexy line, the latest being *Innocent Mistress, Royal Wife*.

I have changed, and so have my books, and my readers. So too have my publishers—now fully computerised! I write to self-imposed deadlines and I email my manuscripts to the publisher, I check the bestseller lists eagerly, and even have a yearly schedule for writing.

However, some things never change. One is the camaraderie I've found among readers and writers in this wonderful genre of ours, and another is a publisher's hunger for intriguing new books to present to the world. Produce a good book, and if a publisher believes he or she can find a place for it in their program, they will publish it.

Good luck.

ROBYN DONALD lives in Northland, New Zealand, close to the beaches of the beautiful Bay of Islands, with her long-suffering husband and a smart, bossy corgi called Buster. When not writing she is busy with family, gardening and writing, but nothing will ever take the place of the joy of opening a new book by a favourite author.

2

LATIN LOVERS
and others

HELEN BIANCHIN

There's something about a foreign hero . . . that dark, faintly brooding quality, with a touch of arrogance. A little bit ruthless, but possessed of integrity. Tall—he should be tall! Good athletic build. Preferably dark-haired, with dark eyes, and sculptured facial features. Wealthy, with all the assets wealth can provide . . . the mansion, luxury car/s, a sizeable sea cruiser, designer clothes. And he *knows* women!

The perfect man.

Well, not quite. He needs a flaw or two. Maybe something from his past has affected his attitude to life. Perhaps he loved and lost, and has become a hardened cynic who mistrusts women in general.

Or possibly he has yet to meet *the* woman who is going to knock him off his feet . . . not literally, but emotionally.

Could be he prefers to play the field, bedding various women and choosing not to marry for whatever reason. Being a hero, he's circumspect, practises safe sex, and ends one relationship before beginning another.

What if he's a bad boy made good? Imagining how he made it from a rough background to the nouveau riche provides numerous possibilities.

And his name . . . it needs to be strong to promote the right image. Change Ralph to Rafael and suddenly a tall, dark Spaniard springs to mind. Or Alejandro, Manolo, Diego. In *Mistress by Contract* I coupled Rafael Velez-Aquilera with Mikayla, and the sparks flew!

Switch Nicholas to Nikolaos and our hero assumes a Greek origin. Or Dimitri, Alexi, Luc, Georgiou. *His Pregnancy Ultimatum* featured Nikolos Karedes and Mia . . . and Nikolos was too hot to handle! French . . . Raoul, Michel, Laz, Sebastien. I had fun with Raoul, Michel and Sebastien, the Lanier brothers, giving each hero his own story, and matching them with strong-minded heroines.

From France, we move to Italy with Stefano, Carlo, Cesare, Marcello. I have a fondness for Cesare Giannelli, for he became the hero in my first book. As the setting was a tobacco farm, it was kind of nice to have a few of my husband's Italian friends query if

I'd modelled Cesare on a *real* person. I managed that one rather well, by assuring them Cesare possessed a combination of all their heroic qualities!

Let's go further east, and mention a sheikh . . . now there's a realm of possibilities!

I dipped my toe in the water with a sheikh plot, and named the hero Shalef bin Youssef Al-Sayed. Bit of a mouthful, but in my mind it portrayed an exceedingly powerful hero. A mix of arrogance, a touch of ruthlessness, intensely sexual and sensual.

It helps if you can have the hero say a word or phrase in his own language . . . just ensure it's correct! *Querida* is Spanish for 'darling'. *Amante is* the Italian equivalent of 'lover', while the French *mon coeur* translates to 'my heart'. The Greek tend to revert to *agape mou* when they refer to their love or lover.

Let's not forget Australian, New Zealand and American heroes. I have a penchant for Jared, Jake, Raf, Dominic, Sloane, Wyatt, Tyler. *The Disobedient Bride* pitted Lianne against Tyler Benedict . . . and yes, Lianne was a tad feisty!

If you need a visual image, there are any number of male actors and models to choose from! A Google or Yahoo search will provide pictures of many handsome hunks . . .

I have to admit I particularly enjoy employing a foreign hero in a story. During my time in far-north Queensland, I became fascinated by the existence of arranged marriages and marriages of convenience among some of my husband's friends—men who'd emigrated from Italy, Greece or Yugoslavia (as it was then) who needed a wife to help manage the farm and the workers, and to cook and clean. My husband and I attended a wedding reception where the marriage was arranged by the families of the bride and groom, who were married by proxy in two different countries. Although the bride and groom had corresponded, they met for the first time when the bride was greeted by her husband at the airport. And yes, mutual respect developed into affection, then love, and the marriage exists to this day.

There were other instances, and I once queried a friend as to what had drawn her to accept an arranged marriage. Her answer provided an interesting perspective. The parents of both families knew and respected each other, she explained, her husband had come from a good, hard-working background, and he would make a good father for their children. *But what of love?* That happens after, she assured me.

It's a theme I've used several times with many variations and twists. I never cease to be intrigued by how a powerful man who has it all can be emotionally undone by a very special woman . . . the *one* above all others. His emotional journey becomes one of self-discovery, a knowledge there is an area of his life he's unable to control. Together with this comes the realisation that his life means little or nothing without her. That what they share is a deep abiding love, in all its many facets.

HERO'S BACKGROUND

Next we need to give the hero an occupation, a career. Entrepreneur covers a lot of ground, but it's good to pin it down . . . Is he a real-estate mogul? CEO of his own company? And if so, what does his company specialise in? Maybe he's an engineering whiz? A computer software designer who's made a fortune? Specialises in high finance? The vintner of a thriving vineyard? The choices are many.

Then there's the location . . . this is where it's fun. If the hero is of Spanish origin, why not use a setting in Spain for part of the book—Madrid, perhaps? What about a vineyard in Tuscany if the hero is Italian? A Greek hero who owns a small Greek island? In North America, there's New York, Chicago . . . I've used each of the above settings. If you haven't visited the location you choose to use, ensure you do your research well!

And let's not forget Australia—home ground. The cities, the outback. The tropical far north. My first book was set on a tobacco farm in Mareeba, where the background was authentic and some of the heroine's encounters with farm life closely mirrored my own. I met and married an Italian from Treviso in northern

Italy, who was share-farming tobacco in Mareeba—but we were poor and lived in rugged barracks in conditions which, when my mother visited, reduced her to tears. Naturally, in line with a Mills & Boon novel, the hero should be wealthy, the house modern and beautifully furnished.

Much depends on the line you choose to write for. Books published under the Harlequin Mills & Boon Presents/Modern/Sexy imprints are known for their focus on glitz, glamour and sophistication. Ideally, a city setting provides the necessary social background . . . but not necessarily for the entire story.

WHAT WILL YOUR MOTHER THINK?

The following is quoted in part from a workshop speech I gave at the Romance Writers of Australia Conference held on the Gold Coast in August 2003. General advice which I feel holds true to the art of portraying passion . . .

As a writer of romance, you're taking the reader by the hand and leading her through a highly evocative, intensely sensual experience. Be very aware of reader anticipation and reader expectation.

It's advisable to lose any inhibitions you may have regarding your nearest and dearest reading your work. That amounts to a mental editor sitting on your shoulder . . . you know the one who whispers *dear heaven, whatever will my mother think if she reads this* in your ear when you've written a particularly evocative scene.

The *focus* is romance, the emphasis is *intimacy*, the key is *emotion*.

What do you want as a reader? I know I want *recognition* of sexual chemistry from the first moment the hero and heroine meet.

I want it to be *electric, magnetic*.

I want the heroine to *know* from the first time she meets the hero that he's dangerous in every way to her emotional peace of mind.

He's going to invade her senses, and turn life as she knows it upside down.

If she lets him.

The *focus* is the development of emotion, sensuality, passion and intimacy between two people, a combination with the power to change lives.

When I began writing in the early 1970s, there were no computers, no internet, and airmail letters took a week to reach Mills & Boon's head office in London. Available guidelines were confined to one page. There were very few national or international writing organisations, and published and aspiring romance writers residing in Australasia were quite isolated.

As an only child in New Zealand, I loved to read and liked nothing better than to curl up comfortably with a book. From Enid Blyton and Nancy Drew to doctor–nurse stories, eventually discovering Mills & Boon as a teenager. Romances . . . I devoured them, for they made much more interesting reading than school textbooks.

Then *life* intervened, as it does, and following four years' legal secretarial work in Auckland, I crossed the Tasman to Melbourne, worked there for eighteen months, then travelled the length and breadth of Australia, and ended up in Mareeba . . . where I met my future husband.

I wrote lots of letters home, and a girlfriend suggested I write a book. The idea was put on hold for a few years . . . *life* again, the birth of a daughter, a shift back to Auckland, the birth of two sons. And yes, I was still reading romances!

I thought I might try to write one. So I bought a portable typewriter, set it up at the end of the dining-room table, and began to write the sort of book I'd most like to read. I didn't tell anyone, and my family thought I was simply writing very long letters to friends! Eventually I sent off the manuscript. It came back, with the editorial comment that it was too short and lacking in sufficient detail, *but* they thought the story had merit, and if I'd care to develop it further, they'd be interested in viewing it again.

What did I do? I put the manuscript at the back of the wardrobe, thinking, *So you thought you could write a book—ha!* Six months later I retrieved and reworked it, then sent it off again. It came back, this time with the editorial comment that it was too long and contained too much extraneous detail. However (lovely word, that!), they were very interested, and if I chose to cut the length a little and remove the extraneous detail, they would like to see it again.

Did I know this was a *good* letter? Not really. But I'd come this far, and I wasn't about to give up. The third attempt was accepted in September 1974 and published in June (on the thirteenth!) 1975. And I had a contract for two more books.

This was serious stuff, I decided, and replaced the portable typewriter with a standard manual. Around the seventh book, we added an extra room onto the house and I had my own home office . . . bliss! I wrote eleven books in New Zealand before we crossed the Tasman again in 1981 and settled in south-east Queensland.

By this time, I thought I had a handle on the writing process—but the images in my head didn't agree.

The hero and heroine in the story were fine with the first chapter . . . once I'd reworked the set-up for the umpteenth time. (I take a l-o-n-g time with the first chapter, and have been known to rewrite it around thirty times. Yes, *thirty!* I counted.)

Okay, once the first chapter is done to my satisfaction, I fall into a lull. The heroine doesn't really want to be bothered with the second chapter . . . she wants to skip to the *interesting* part (and read into that what you will!); she wants excitement, action.

But hey, I'm not up to that part yet. And I should write the book sequentially from beginning to end. At least, that's what I believed to be the *right* way to create a book.

So I bought how-to-write books and studied them. Most were wordy, some were very technical . . . I absorbed them all, and endeavoured to persist with some of the recommendations. Except each of my heroines failed to conform, and the heroes tended to become antsy.

Then I read an article on making movies, which explained how a movie is shot in *scenes*. What's more, those scenes are frequently filmed out of sequence.

It was a revelation. That was how I instinctively *wanted* to write. Set up the beginning, then create the scenes.

What's more, *in my mind that's how I viewed each scene—like a technicolour movie*. The location; the hero and heroine as actors playing their part. Even down to what they wear. I also *hear* what they say—the voice, its tone and depth—like a soundtrack running through my head.

Many how-to books state *there are no rules* in writing a novel.

Either a writer is a pantser (doesn't plan, and flies by the seat of his/her pants), or a writer is a plotter (plans in detail). There is a third: a combination pantser and plotter.

It's here that I must add a note of caution. If you're a pantser, writing in scenes (unless you write them sequentially) will merely aid confusion and generally won't work. If you're a plotter, then you might care to try writing in scenes.

I have to admit it took me a while to reach my current method, which I'm happy to share. It works well for me . . . and it may work for you.

THE FIRST STEPS

First is the choice of theme: a marriage of convenience, hero/heroine wronged who sets out to exact revenge, hidden baby, heroine tames bad-boy hero, separated hero/heroine reunited by an act of Fate. These are just a few, each of which I've used, employing a new twist, a different slant.

I key in a character biography: names, ages, physical description, eye colour (can't have blue eyes in the first chapter becoming brown in chapter three!), occupation; where the hero and heroine reside—whether I plan for the hero to own a penthouse apartment, mansion or villa . . . likewise the heroine; the vehicle they each drive. Minor characters follow. I decide on the season.

By this time I have a loose (*very* loose) idea, together with a picture in my head. Then I create a synopsis in draft, perhaps three or four pages, using a coloured felt pen to highlight the important points, and let it simmer in my mind for a day or two. When I think I've got a handle on the direction I want to take—or shall we amend that to *where the characters will lead me*—I'll expand the draft synopsis until I've developed the story in more detail— probably around twelve single-spaced pages.

Allow a little mulling time . . . sounds like mulled wine, doesn't it? . . . then comes the fun part. I sit with the twelve single-spaced pages and divide the draft into anywhere between fifteen and twenty scenes. I number and name each one in sequence as a separate file on the computer.

After this I work at setting up the first chapter: writing, rewriting, deleting, adding, enhancing, revising . . . all of these, until I'm happy the first chapter is as *right* as I can make it.

KANGAROO-HOPPING

At this point I check out the draft copy of scenes . . . and it's usually my heroine who decides *which* scene she wants me to work on. *That* one looks interesting, she tells me . . . the hero is being ruthlessly autocratic, and she's in the mood to verbally best him. *And she does, beautifully!*

And so the story continues, scene by scene, and most often out of sequence (I fondly term this 'kangaroo-hopping'). Occasionally inspiration will strike as to how I'll wrap up the final chapter, and the images will be so vivid I'll go ahead and write the final chapter, rather than make copious notes.

Each scene will occupy anything from a half-chapter to an entire chapter, which I'll edit, expanding or minimising as I feel necessary. The already completed first chapter becomes the main manuscript document, and I insert each numbered scene into the main document as I complete it. When all the scenes are inserted into the main document numerically in sequence, I then need to write linking passages to ensure an ongoing flow.

Once the manuscript is fully edited, I read it through on-screen, make any adjustments and corrections, then print out a hard copy. That's when I clear the desk, sit with red pen in hand, reference my character biography printout and my original draft synopsis where I've highlighted important points in the story, and do a tick-check that I've covered everything.

At this stage I ensure I have uninterrupted time to read the printed manuscript from beginning to end, *slowly and thoroughly.* The next day I do another read-through, this time at normal reading speed. By then I'm reasonably confident the manuscript is ready to be sent to my editor.

Following a week or two of catching up on everyday life, there is the need to begin seriously considering what I'll write next. And the process begins again.

DESCRIBING LATIN LOVERS

It's not *enough* to say the hero is a tall, attractive man with brown eyes. In a romance, the reader wants *more*.

To give an example, the following is taken from my book, *Purchased: His Perfect Wife*:

Two men rose to their feet, and Lara acknowledged the lawyer, offered an apology, then turned slightly towards the tall, broad-shouldered, impeccably tailored figure silhouetted against floor-to-ceiling glass, met a pair of dark, enigmatic grey eyes, and inclined her head.

'Wolfe.'

'Lara.' His voice was a smooth, slightly accented drawl, and she endeavoured to control the nervous tension he managed to arouse without any seeming effort at all.

There was something vaguely primitive apparent, an electric, almost raw sexuality that was

dangerous to any woman's peace of mind . . .
especially hers.

PASSION

Mention Latin lovers, and *passion* in all its variations
inevitably follows!

Picture an attractive Spaniard (I'll leave you to
choose), with liquid dark eyes and a sexy smile . . . he's
utterly gorgeous, and has *the* look. You know the one.
It melts a woman's heart, seeps into her soul, and her
imagination soars off the Richter scale as she wonders
what he'd be like as a lover—especially *hers*.

The French language of love spoken softly with great
emotion by a wonderfully sensual Frenchman . . . and
wow, the female heart races to a faster beat.

A good example can be found in *The Martinez
Marriage Revenge*, which was published in April 2008.
The back-cover blurb reads:

When Shannay's marriage to billionaire Marcello
Martinez ended, she returned home hoping
never to see her husband again. But she carried
with her a precious secret . . . Now, four years
later, Marcello has tracked his wife down and
discovered that she has hurt him in the cruellest
of ways . . . by keeping knowledge of his child

from him! Marcello is determined that Shannay will pay for her behaviour—and what better way than returning to their marital home . . . and their marriage bed?

Here's a scene from chapter 6, p. 75:

He lowered his head down to hers and captured her mouth with his own in a hard kiss that took her by surprise and plundered at will.

The faint cry of distress rose and died in her throat, and almost as if he sensed it his touch gentled a little and became frankly sensual, seeking the sensitive tissues before stroking the edge of her tongue with the tip of his own in a flagrant dance that stirred at the latent passion simmering beneath the surface of her control.

She felt his hands shift as one slid to cup the back of her head, while the other smoothed down her back and brought her close against him.

Her eyelids shuttered down as she fought against capitulation. The temptation to return his kiss was unbearable, and she groaned as he eased back and began a sensual tasting, teasing the soft fullness of her lower lip, nipping a little with the edges of his teeth, until she succumbed to the sweet sorcery he bestowed.

Dear heaven. It was like coming home as he shaped her mouth with his own, encouraging her response, taking her with him in an evocative tasting that became *more* . . . and promised much.

Her breasts firmed against his chest, their sensitive peaks hardening in need . . . for the touch of his hand, his mouth, and she whimpered, totally lost in the moment.

The hardness of his erection was a potent force, and warmth raced through her veins, activating each pleasure pulse until she felt so incredibly sensually *alive*, it was almost impossible not to beg.

Equally important is the need to wrap up the story with a declaration of love in the final chapter. The reader really wants a satisfactory ending . . . that *aah* moment derived from the final pages.

Again, an example from *Purchased: His Perfect Wife*:

'I thought I had it all,' Wolfe began quietly. 'Until you came into my life and brought the sun, the moon . . . everything that matters.' He trailed light fingers across her collarbone, then traced the soft hollow at the base of her throat. 'You confronted me on every level. Argued, and put me firmly in my place.' He shook his head.

'So fiercely independent . . . I was torn between wringing your neck or taking you hard and fast until you begged for mercy.' And he had . . . more than once.

'You crept beneath my skin, in a way no other woman ever did.' He traced the outline of her lips, and smiled as he felt them tremble beneath his touch. 'I went to New York alone, thinking some space and distance would provide some perspective. All it proved was how much I missed you.' His lips teased her temple, then settled at a sensitive pulse beneath her ear. 'You weren't there when I reached out in the night.' His warm breath slid over the surface of her skin as he sought the edge of her mouth. 'Or in the pre-dawn hours. The apartment which had never seemed empty or lonely before, became somewhere I didn't want to be. All I could think of every waking minute was you. The sound of your laughter, the way you smile, and how your eyes light up at the smallest pleasure.' He eased both hands over her shoulders, and shaped her arms until he reached her hands, then he threaded his fingers through her own and lifted their joined hands to his lips. 'How you feel in my arms when we make love.'

Boneless, she registered dimly. And melting. His.

'My wife . . . a young woman I'd initially regarded as a convenient possession for whom I thought respect and affection was enough.

'How wrong could I be? You became so much a part of me. The other half of my soul. You, Lara. Only you.'

She held on to his hands, afraid if she let go she'd fall into an ignominious puddle at his feet.

The one thing she'd wished for . . . the only thing that mattered . . . was hers. Gifted willingly and without demur.

The most important gift of all. Love everlasting.

A lifetime. She'd make sure of it.

And so, she knew in her heart, would he.

USEFUL REFERENCE BOOKS

The following books are some of a few I've found particularly helpful:

Goal, Motivation and Conflict: The Building Blocks of Good Fiction by Debra Dixon (Gryphon Books for Writers, 1996).

Eats, Shoots & Leaves: The Zero Tolerance Approach to Punctuation by Lynne Truss (Profile Books, 2003).

Save The Cat: The Last Book on Screenwriting You'll Ever Need by Blake Snyder (Michael Wiese Productions, 2005).

Writing the Breakout Novel: Winning Advice from a Top Agent and His Bestselling Client by Donald Maass (Writers Digest Books, 2002).

The Career Novelist: A Literary Agent Offers Strategies for Success by Donald Maass (Heinemann, 1996).

HELEN BIANCHIN worked as a legal secretary in her native New Zealand, then spent two years travelling and working in Australia, where she met and married her Italian-born husband in the northern Queensland tobacco-farming town of Mareeba. This meant a 180-degree lifestyle change: cooking for seasonal workers, helping out on the farm, and caring for hundreds of chickens, ducks and turkeys. Should she mention she also had to kill, clean and prepare chickens for the table?

After three years Helen, her husband and their daughter moved to New Zealand, where they added two sons to their family, and the tentative idea of writing a romance novel emerged. Writers are advised to 'write what you know', so Helen created an Italian-born hero who owned a prosperous tobacco farm, meshing fact with fiction and authenticity!

Six years after her first book was published, Helen and her family returned to Australia to settle in south-east Queensland, where they currently reside. Their adult children, together with six young grandchildren live close by.

Helen's interests include a love of reading, seeing movies and watching television. She enjoys catching up with friends, and has a long-standing affection for animals, especially cats.

At present she owns two beautiful Birmans, one of which insists on sharing her desk for an hour or two each day!

Helen's books have appeared on the *USA Today*, Nielsen BookScan and Waldenbooks bestseller lists. She is currently working on her fifty-seventh title.

3

PACKING AN *emotional punch*

VALERIE PARV

What do editors mean when they say your writing lacks emotional depth, or needs more emotional punch? Isn't your heroine falling to the ground, bewailing the loss of the home she loves? Isn't your hero gritting his teeth as he fights for truth and justice?

Writing my first romance novels, I also believed that poignant descriptions of physical responses and heroic deeds translated into emotional punch. So why did editors say I was telling, rather than showing? And that my stories, page-turning as they were, needed greater emotional depth?

I should have suspected something was wrong when

the first time I was seriously kissed I was told to 'put some feeling into it'.

Unbeknown to me, I was writing *about* emotions without feeling them inside myself. Growing up as I did in a socially dysfunctional family was a sure way to wall off all the extremes of emotion. My parents elevated not getting angry to an art form, which meant, according to a counsellor I consulted, that both ends of the spectrum became unsafe territory—joy and passion as well as the negative emotions. As the saying goes, 'You can't have one without the other'. It wasn't until I learned it's not only okay to get angry, but essential for mental and spiritual health, that I was able to explore a full range of emotional responses. The more I got in touch with my own emotions, the more clearly I could see where I needed to go in my books. You can't write what you don't feel.

The same problem comes up again and again when I'm judging the final entries in the Valerie Parv Award, a contest run annually by Romance Writers of Australia and named in my honour. Time and again, the entries demonstrate powerful writing voices, while the ingenious storytelling keeps me turning pages. But all too often, we fail to see how the characters really feel about their situation and each other. The author may well tell us in various ways, but we aren't in there having the experience for ourselves.

CATHARSIS

A good definition of emotional depth is where readers feel they are sharing in the character's experiences. The Ancient Greeks called this 'catharsis', an emotional outlet provided by a drama. When we cry with a fictional heroine, we release some of our own stored-up sorrow. The same with joy. We may come away from the experience feeling emotionally wrung-out, but also cleansed and liberated—which tells us that emotion on the page is there to evoke emotion in the reader. But how can a writer make a reader feel anything?

First, you have to make readers care about your characters. This means, first and foremost, the author must know them as people. We've all had the experience of watching news footage of a horrendous plane crash on the other side of the world. We feel sad for the people concerned, but from an emotional distance. But what happens if some of the passengers are from your own city? Right away there's a stronger sense of connection with their plight, the reason most news reports specifically mention if any local people are involved. In practice, the crash will rarely rate much airtime *unless* locals are on the scene.

What if some of your family members were among the passengers? The connection then becomes personal. You're likely to switch channels constantly, searching for every scrap of information, and spend hours calling hotlines for reassurance that your loved ones are okay. You've gone from an emotional distance to total empathy with the crash victims. When fiction achieves the same empathy, it has that all-important emotional punch.

POINT OF VIEW

The reader needs to feel as if this story is about her. She is the heroine, suffering through the pangs of falling in love and having her heart's desire thwarted by the problem keeping the hero and heroine apart. This is what's meant by point of view (POV)—the person through whose eyes you want the reader to experience the story; the viewpoint character. This character is the reader's gateway into the romance. You want them to step into the heroine's body and experience the story first-hand, rather than being told about it by you, the author. You do this by immersing the reader in the viewpoint character's emotional responses to what's happening in the story.

At every step of the story, you need to ask yourself how the viewpoint character *feels* about what's happening. Don't let yourself back off or skim the surface. Dig and dig inside yourself for the emotions you would feel in the same situation then drag them out onto the page through the five senses: sight, sound, smell, taste and touch. This doesn't mean every event needs to be expressed through all five, as long as you keep in mind that our senses are how we 'read' the world. Giving the reader sensory clues to how the viewpoint character feels will enable them to feel as if they're taking part in the story. .

As I learned, the only way to do this is by dropping your emotional guard. Remember, you can't write what you don't feel. Before you can share the character's emotions, you need to be in touch with your own. This means checking out all your feelings and memories, even if they're not particularly pleasant, with a professional counsellor if need be. The fewer emotional barriers you have, the more ways your characters will have to respond to events. When you can cry with them, sigh with them, get aroused with them and rage with them, then you're sufficiently inside their feelings to share them with your readers in rich, sensory detail.

One of the most valuable tips I got as a writer came from the late Frank Brennan, half of the original Emma Darcy writing team. Aware of my struggle to get inside my characters, he advised me to 'put in as much emotion as you think you need then double it'.

At first, this advice made little sense. Wasn't I wallowing in all this emotional 'stuff'? Couldn't we just get on with the story? Wasn't it enough to say the heroine was afraid, maybe mention her trembling hand as she reached for a weapon, and the effort she made to slow her racing heartbeat, then show the battle with the bad guys, with the hero at her side? Sure, all of that was useful. In a mainstream thriller, it may even be enough.

But we're talking romance, and the reader wants to step into the heroine's shoes. How do you want them to feel? What past experiences does the fictional situation bring up for the reader? If your heroine is defeated, she loses more than her freedom. She loses any chance of a future with the man she's come to love. If she achieves her goal, things may become even worse for her. If their goals are opposed, he's going to ride off into the sunset and she'll never see him again.

This is emotion at work. It's the push–pull of wanting something desperately; of striving for high ideals and fearing you'll fall short; of having desires at odds with those of the one you love, so there seems no hope of a happy ending.

As an editor at a recent writing conference expressed it, you want the reader to be so caught up in the emotional struggle that she flips to the back of the book to reassure herself the heroine makes it safely to the end. Whew. Reassured, she can then go back and suffer with the heroine through all the trials and stresses needed to reach that happy ending.

SUFFERING IS GOOD

Suffering is a good word to use when discussing emotional punch. A lot of emotional tension in a novel comes from the characters' suffering. It's sometimes described as getting your characters up a tree, then throwing rocks at them. How will they handle the obstacles put in their way? You or I might be tempted to give in or fall apart. Your characters should be far more noble than us. They are how we wish we could be in similar straits. They will fight to the bitter end for what they care about.

If they give in, it will be for noble reasons. The heroine sees how dedicated the hero is to his medical missionary work, and will walk away rather than make him choose between her and his work. He will come to know that she's reluctant to commit to a relationship because her last experience ended so badly. Her husband and child both died. How can she risk losing so much ever again?

Both characters must compromise to have what they want most: each other's love. The hero might decide to continue his medical mission in his own country, where marriage isn't such an obstacle. She might discover that it really is better to have loved and lost than never to have loved at all. The memories of her first relationship and her precious child will always be with her. The hero will honour them as much as she does, while showing her that a new love is no less wonderful for being different from the old. We will be along for the ride as they give each other new meaning and hope for the future.

WHY EMOTIONS MATTER

Emotions are universal. They are the motivation behind nearly all human interactions: the reason why people are willing to die for a cause; why mothers will do just about anything for their children; why people kill.

The motivation might be love, passion for a cause, need (usually based on fear of being deprived), the desire for revenge when we feel we've been wronged in some way, even—some think—a biological drive which goes deeper than our own need for survival. This can certainly be seen in the heroism and sacrifice of a mother defending her child.

It's hard to involve readers emotionally in a conflict such as 'will he or won't he destroy the rainforest'. You need to create a conflict which brings your characters' emotions into collision. One character's wants should be at odds with what the other character wants, usually described as conflict. Emotional wants spring from feelings we hold towards something—a need, or a lack, a wish to hold onto something or someone being threatened, a hurt needing revenge.

In a romance novel, the emotional conflict does not arise from whether or not these two will fall in love. Or whether one loves and the other doesn't. In a romance, the love they both feel is a given from the outset. The moment they set eyes on each other, they feel an almost overwhelming attraction. If they could simply give in to their feelings, the book would be over on page one.

Therefore something must come between them. Whether you call it a conflict, tension or problem, the something needs to be huge, and above all, emotion-based rather than a misunderstanding they could clear up in a few words, such as mistaken identity—he's kissing a woman who turns out to be his sister. Giving your characters a passion—for life, an ideal, a lover— makes them admirable, and invites us to get caught up in their struggles. The higher and more important the stakes they're reaching for, the more strongly we'll want them to succeed.

A child in jeopardy, a longed-for baby, financial ruin, a good reputation under threat, are all personal issues growing from inside the characters, from who they are, their family backgrounds and experiences. If his experiences and history are very different from hers, you have the potential for emotion-based or internal conflict. For example, if he grew up in an abusive family, he may have decided never to bring children into the world. Finding that he has fathered a child provides huge potential for conflict. He may want to provide for the child financially while keeping his emotional distance, while the heroine wants him to be involved with his child.

Alternatively, the heroine may be opposed to marrying, having experienced the pain of her parents' messy divorce, as well as having been cheated on by a man in her adult life. If the hero proposes marriage to provide a family for his child, the heroine may resist, agreeing only under limited conditions which will, themselves, provide strong emotion-based conflict.

The more attracted the two are to each other, the more affected they will be by the problem keeping them apart. Strong conflicts generate strong emotions. Your job is to make the reader care about your characters and want them to reach their happy ending. Take a look at the problem you've raised between them. Can you imagine a reader flipping to the end of your book for reassurance that everything will end happily?

BACKGROUND AND HISTORY

The emotions your characters experience will differ according to the backgrounds you create for them. Depending on who we are and where we come from, we all react differently to stress in our lives. Some people laugh, some cry, some get angry. Others overexercise or overeat. Some people prefer to talk through their problems, others bury them in frantic activity or withdrawal. In order to know how your character will react, you need to discover their dominant emotion. This isn't just a label you place on them, but a conclusion you reach through exploring their backgrounds.

The conclusion people reach about themselves, usually in early childhood, is often described as a core decision (CD). Depending on how we're treated by our caregivers, this core decision might be that we're clever and entertaining, or, more commonly, clumsy, stupid or ugly. This immature decision then becomes a lens through which we view the world, shaping our behaviour—sometimes for life.

While studying for my counselling diploma, I learned that we often arrange our lives to prove these early beliefs about ourselves. If we decide we're stupid, we might not try hard enough to achieve good grades. If we think we're unlovable, we'll unconsciously choose partners who won't stick around, 'proving' our core beliefs.

Working out your characters' core decisions ensures they'll have believable backgrounds and consistent actions. The decision should be framed in 'I talk'. Not 'love doesn't last' but 'I can't love because it only ends in disaster'.

A heroine with this core belief might have dated love 'em and leave 'em types in the past, validating her core decision. Then along comes the hero who attracts her strongly, while her CD is telling her he'll leave like the others she's known. Allowing herself intimacy with the hero is a huge risk because her experience tells her it won't last. Something has to happen at the climax of the story to change her CD forever. The hero also needs a CD, preferably conflicting with the heroine's CD.

Creating a detailed biography of each character, including their family history, will help you determine their core decisions and how these might come into conflict. This also helps you decide on details— such as setting and plot—which work with these characterisations.

PUTTING IN THE EMOTION

Consider this example from one of my workshops. The scene is dramatic enough, but has almost no emotional content.

> Jenny closed the phone, hardly able to believe what she'd just heard. Blake was already married?
>
> Blake looked up from his laptop. 'Who was that, darling?'
>
> She hesitated only a moment. 'Your wife.'

Workshop participants are asked to rewrite the scene, supplying the missing emotions. In one example, we may see that Jenny is the home-making type, baking bread, imagining herself the perfect wife—a far cry from the 'other woman'.

Jenny's hand shook as she closed the phone, the woman's voice ringing in her ears. 'He's my husband, you homewrecker.'

Homewrecker? How could she be? The aroma of baking bread assailed her from the kitchen, the mouthwatering promise mocking her. She had thought she was making a home, and now . . .

Her inner chill was accentuated by the ripples of air from the overhead fan. Calm down, she told herself. She had to think this through.

Blake—or was he a stranger she only thought she knew—looked up from his laptop, then set it aside and came to her, frowning as she recoiled from his outstretched hand. 'You're shaking, darling. What was it, an obscene phone call?'

Of course it was obscene. Discovering that the man she loved might be already married plunged her thoughts into turmoil. 'You could say so,' she whispered. 'It was your wife.'

This exercise shows how your character could react, depending on her history and core decision. It's easy to imagine this Jenny as having been brought up in a home where everyone had their role. Her mother possibly cooked, and there was no whiff of marital disharmony.

Unless . . . her upbringing went another way. Say she'd been exposed to her parents' arguments and resulting family chaos. Her core decision might be that it isn't safe to build a life around another person. Getting involved with Blake involved some emotional risk-taking on her part. In this situation, the phone call threatens to 'prove' her core belief, reminding her strongly of a past she'd resolved to avoid for herself. Thus, the scene might read:

> Jenny's hand shook as she closed the phone, the stranger's voice ringing in her ears. 'He's my husband, you homewrecker.'
>
> Homewrecker. How many times had she heard that word tossed between her parents, more hurtful than the crockery they'd also hurled. Her mother's boyfriends pitted against his office romances, until Jenny had felt relieved when they had their day in court and the hating could stop. Except it hadn't. She'd lived with her mother, who never stopped reminding her that men were high risk. Jenny should have known better than to build her dream life around Blake.

He put his laptop aside and came to her, frowning as she recoiled from his outstretched hand. 'You're shaking, darling. What was it, an obscene caller?'

No, she thought with a deepening feeling of doom. 'I should have known this was too good to be true.'

'What is?'

Her gesture took in the cosy apartment. 'This. The sweet words, the promises. I should have listened to my mother.'

'Was that her on the phone?'

Her laugh grated in her ears. 'Hardly. It was your wife.'

In each case, the heroine reacts differently according to her emotional make-up. She's responding out of deep feelings, and what she decides to do next will also be emotion-based. The situation is the scene in the apartment, followed by the phone call. The emotional punch comes from how the heroine, as viewpoint character, deals with the situation.

The possibility of Blake being married is an example of external conflict, which is generated by the plot you weave around the characters. The internal conflict is created by their reactions to finding themselves in this predicament. Depending on their core decision, some people wouldn't care if their partner were married or not, providing they're free to pursue a relationship. Others would make more of having been lied to over the issue, if—as in my family—lying was considered a hanging offence. Or the heroine might have total faith in Blake and think the woman caller was lying to cause trouble between them.

In the first example, we don't hear Blake's side of the story, but his history may have included a hysterical mother who accused her loving husband of having affairs with no evidence, leading Blake to believe that no amount of reassurance would convince Jenny he was loyal, and that the woman caller was a crank. He may well walk out of the situation, leaving her to think what she chooses.

In the second example, if Blake was the product of a stable, loving home, he may have known Jenny was emotionally vulnerable about relationships, and intended to explain about his failed marriage after he'd convinced Jenny not all families were like hers.

As you can see, the situation is only a set of circumstances you create between your characters. How they react depends on who they are as individuals and the core decisions they are operating from. This is what makes the story compelling and different. By choosing a situation with built-in emotional possibilities, you create emotional tension between the characters until the reader starts turning pages to find out how—or if—the conflict is resolved so the characters can have their happy ending.

If you'd chosen a less emotion-based conflict, the scene could have gone very differently. Jenny could believe Blake shared her concern for homeless people, and have set aside a valuable piece of land on which to build a much-needed shelter. The caller might be the owner of a company who has engaged Blake's consultancy to build her headquarters on the site. A conflict over whether a shelter or a high-rise ends up on a piece of land is frequently the kind many new writers choose, yet it carries far less intrinsic emotional punch. You can try to draw emotions into the deal by showing Jenny as a believer in equality and fairness, but what does that make Blake?

If you like, play with the phone-call scene between Jenny and Blake, exploring more emotion-based possibilities.

STRANGER THAN FICTION

When I do these exercises in workshops, participants sometimes put forward a situation with plenty of complications but little emotional punch—like the one above, where Blake plans to develop Jenny's precious rainforest. Or they'll come up with a story from their own or a friend's experiences. When asked to dig for the emotional content, they'll be reluctant, insisting that the story 'really happened' the way they're telling it.

While our own experiences give us lots of ideas, real-life events don't always make for the most emotional stories. Oddly enough, they may not be believable, even if they really took place. We've all heard the saying about truth being stranger than fiction. What I suggest you do is look to your own experiences for ideas, but don't write about them exactly the way they happened. Instead, search for the emotional basis of the event.

For example, when I was growing up my family moved around a lot. What does this mean in emotional terms? I was always the new kid on the block, trying to make a place for myself in a new environment. My readers may have lived in the same house most of their lives, but I'll bet they've had the experience of being the odd one out in a group, wanting desperately to fit in, to belong.

By getting to the core of the emotion, the need to belong, I'm able to share a universal experience with the reader. It's the same with loss. Perhaps you've never lost someone really close to you. But you will have lost someone or something in your life. How did you feel? What emotions do you experience now, thinking about your loss? By endowing your characters with those same emotions, but in the context of an entirely fictitious loss, you create the all-important gateway through which your reader can enter your story.

For practice, I suggest you think of an incident in your childhood. Write down what happened, then try to pin down the emotion behind it. How did it make you feel? Rather than using the real event in your book, give your characters the emotion in response to their unique situation.

The most successful fiction, television and movies are all emotion-based. Take the 1982 movie, *E.T.: The Extra-Terrestrial*. On the surface, this story is about an alien stranded on Earth and experiencing life with a human family. Emotionally, it's really about enormous loss, homesickness, and being a stranger in a strange land. Stories about superheroes resonate so strongly because they're only superficially about beings with extraordinary powers. On an emotional level, they're about our own core belief that there's more inside us than the world normally sees.

EMOTIONAL STRUCTURE

Another way to ensure your story is emotion-based is to look at the role each scene or chapter is playing in the developing romance. This is best done when you have a completed rough draft or a detailed outline so you can see how the pattern of the relationship is unfolding.

The emotional structure might follow these steps:

- First meeting shows powerful awareness of each other while sowing the seeds of the conflict, the reason why they can't give in to their attraction.

- Admiration, liking complicated by the conflict.
- Close encounter(s); she's fighting her desires while reminding herself of the conflict yet to be resolved.
- Conflict grows despite the close encounters. They fight the passion, lust or desire they feel.
- Lovemaking, often regretted when the conflict seems stronger than before.
- He may declare his feelings but she suspects his motives.
- Despair when the conflict looks insurmountable.
- A future together seems impossible. A decision to resolve the conflict even at the cost of a happy ending.
- The decision proves to be the right one. They are free to commit to each other.

You may have more or fewer steps than these, depending on the length of your book. The couple may or may not make love, again depending on what is acceptable for your readership. But the steps will always work from the least (attraction) to the most powerful (the readiness to sacrifice everything for the beloved). It's a ballet of feelings versus obstacles. You want the reader to worry that *this time* everything won't work out for the best. Remember, love is not the problem—it's the solution. The more strongly the characters are attracted, the more challenging must be the conflict, to the point where it seems insurmountable. There seems no way it can be solved, and without a resolution, there can be no happy ending.

Not all writers agree, but I believe there's a difference between what you share with the reader about your characters, and what they tell each other. My favourite example is Mary Higgins Clark's book, *Where Are the Children?* The heroine, once cleared of causing the disappearance of her children, adopts a new identity, marries again and has a new family. When these children also disappear, the reader would be justified in blaming the heroine. Empathising with a character capable of such horror would be difficult, so the author gives us readers something she doesn't give the characters in the book—the awareness that someone evil is watching the heroine. Knowing this, we empathise more strongly with the heroine as she fights suspicion, and we fear the real culprit will escape justice yet again.

SEXUAL TENSION

Sexual tension is another form of conflict. Any woman who allows this kind of intimacy is making herself vulnerable. She might want intimacy with the hero, but she won't let it happen until she feels there's a chance to resolve their differences. You need to let the tension build and build between them until the reasons for making love become stronger than the problem keeping them apart.

As before, you build the emotional tension by letting the reader share the heroine's feelings (or the hero's) every step of the way. You can show her misgivings by describing what she's feeling, the thoughts going through her mind, the doubts and fears playing against the intense physical need he arouses in her.

Because of the conflict, giving in to her feelings involves a struggle. When she lets it happen, she may be furious with herself on finding the conflict is still there. Or she may feel that the lovemaking has put the relationship on a new, more promising footing—only to find that, if anything, things are worse than before. Now she not only has to deal with the conflict, but also with the emotional consequences of opening herself up to the hero.

How does she feel about this? If she discovers the hero has apparently lied to her, how does she feel? Does the discovery confirm her worst suspicions about him? Or has she let herself trust him and now feels betrayed? Rather than provide a series of incidents, your plot should provide these emotional moments and explore them through the emotional responses of your characters.

Remember, all conflict grows from feelings. Your plot brings your characters together and forces them to interact, but the emotional punch comes from dealing with their feelings. The ideal plot keeps them together as much of the time as possible, so they have no choice but to confront these feelings.

When it comes to your readers, we're often advised to make them laugh, make them cry and make them wait. To this, I urge you to add another vital ingredient: make them feel. Make them long to share the emotional journey as the characters overcome their problems and earn the ultimate reward—the true love and happiness they've struggled long and hard to earn.

VALERIE PARV's books have sold more than twenty-six million copies internationally, and have been translated into over twenty languages, from Russian to Japanese and Icelandic. With a master of arts from Queensland University of Technology and a diploma in professional counselling, she conducts seminars and workshops on creativity and the writer's craft. Her practical guide to the romance genre, *The Art of Romance Writing*, was voted the most useful book on writing in a poll of members of Romance Writers of Australia. A successful writer of non-fiction before turning to romantic suspense, Valerie says she began writing to see *if* she could do it. The challenge looks like keeping her busy for a long time to come.

4

CROSSING THE LINES
and getting it right

LILIAN DARCY

When most readers go into a bookstore, they don't take a lot of notice of who publishes the book they're browsing through or looking for, they just want to buy the darn thing. They take even less notice of what imprint the book is published under. One thing that regular readers of series romance are much more aware of, however, is *lines*. They may not use this word. They're more likely to say, 'the ones with the purple covers', 'the Silhouette Special Edition', or 'the medical romances'. But they know that when they pick up any book with a particular look—the purple cover, the word *Sexy* emblazoned on the front—they're being promised certain ingredients.

For an aspiring writer targeting a particular romance line—or, for that matter, a particular publisher's imprint —or for a seasoned writer looking to expand their range or move into new territory, it's crucial to understand what those ingredients are.

A mistake many writers make is trying to identify various ingredients too schematically and rigidly, often based on too small a sampling of the books. For example, someone might read three books from the Special Edition line, each of which happens to feature a sole parent struggling to raise a young child on the family ranch, and conclude that young children and American ranch settings are non-negotiable ingredients in the mix.

Wider reading of the line would show that it's not the kids and cattle that are the essentials but something less tangible—perhaps the sense of an emotional journey and a woman's search for who she is and where she really belongs. This is the real key. What is the *feel* of each line, imprint or sub-genre? What is the emotional tone? What are the values underlying the hero's or heroine's behaviour? What experiences are the books delivering to the reader? These are often subtle and hard to put into words. Publishers' marketing teams spend months trying to distil this feel into the right colours, fonts, graphics and buzz words that will leap out at the reader and assure them on a subliminal level that they're getting what they want. None of us can afford to think that getting a handle on these flavours is easy.

WRITING VOICE

Another common mistake is to try to squeeze one's writing voice into a shape that it doesn't fit, usually based on assumptions, whether accurate or not, about 'what sells'. The truth here is pretty simple: it can't be done. To a very large extent, our writing voice is something we're stuck with.

All right, so what do we mean by *voice*? Again, it's about flavour and instinct, and it's not something that's easily defined or described. Words like racy, warm, hard-edged, plain-spoken, flamboyant and sophisticated come to mind as possible ways to describe the work of certain authors, but no two writers are alike. One author's *passionate* voice might be quite different to another's, even if the word 'passionate' can describe them both. As well, there will be more than one aspect to any given writer's voice. Janet Evanovich is sassy, funny and fast. Helen Bianchin is languorous and lush. The ingredients and flavours—those words again—are complex.

Like many writers, I took a long time to find and define my own voice and my strengths. I found it rather like listening to a recording of myself speaking. 'Is that really me?' We don't hear ourselves accurately. We're sometimes surprised by what others perceive about how we sound and who we are.

I knew that I liked to create vivid word pictures and infuse my books with a strong sense of life's complex and sometimes unexpected beauty, but it wasn't until editors and friends started telling me, 'Your characters are so real' and 'I love the detail and emotion in your books', that I began to understand what others saw in my voice and style. In my writing, the words and details aren't an end in themselves; they're there to create characters and emotional situations that readers respond to.

Working out where we fit as writers is an important part of any writing journey, especially in the field of popular fiction, where genre boundaries—though they may subtly shift with each new trend—are often quite clearly drawn, and where editors are always looking for something fresh and new, but won't know what it is until they see it. It can take time and many false starts, dead-end roads and uncompleted experiments to work out who we are.

FROM READER TO WRITER

I usually advise new writers to begin this particular journey with the question: *What do I like to read?* This can be a very good guide. If you love to read about commanding, sexy, powerful men then it's more likely you'll be able to write them successfully than if you find yourself tearing up the book you're reading every time its billionaire hero comes out with one of his arrogant, impossible demands. It's not an infallible guide, however. Writers are often swept away in their reading by things they can't write themselves. There's an admiration factor involved. An emotional, character-focused writer can be enthralled by clever, intricate plotting. A pacy thriller writer tries to pull apart another author's finely drawn, true-to-life characters—like pulling apart a clockwork toy to see how it's made—and ends up stumped. *How does she do that?*

On the other hand, if there's a particular sub-genre you absolutely loathe reading, this is a more reliable indication of where you *shouldn't* be aiming to fit. If you've never met a vampire, werewolf or shape-shifter you could like, steer clear of the paranormal genre no matter how many authors are hitting the bestseller lists with these books. If historical detail makes you yawn whether it's collated in a factual book about seventeenth-century English costume or seamlessly woven into a Regency romance, you should probably stick with writing a contemporary story.

Some writers seem to find their niche much more easily than others. If you're one of those, then you're very lucky. Many of us take a long time and generate thousands of unpublishable words before we work out that our strength is character and atmosphere, a lyrical voice, or steamy sex scenes. In fact, I'm still struggling to answer certain questions about who I am as a writer.

When I was writing for Silhouette Romance and looking to move into a second Silhouette line, I told my editor that I'd like to try writing for what was then known as Silhouette Intimate Moments. She looked at me thoughtfully for a moment with her head tilted to one side and said, 'You know, I really see you much more in Special Edition.' She was right, of course. I admired the edgy, plot-driven stories in Intimate Moments (now Silhouette Romantic Suspense) but would have struggled enormously to emulate them. When you receive this kind of feedback from someone whose judgement you trust, grab it with both hands.

At the moment I'm working on a longer book in which romance only forms one thread of the story, and it's a little scary how clueless I often feel about what I'm writing. Is the pacing right? Is the story too complex? Is there enough change and growth in the characters? Do I want the book to be seen as literary fiction, or will it have a wide commercial appeal? I'm too close to the book to really see it. It may take some distance and time, as well as feedback from friends who read it, to work out where it needs to be strengthened and changed.

READING BETWEEN THE LINES

Once you have a clear idea about where you fit—perhaps in your first attempt to become a romance author or in your move to a new sub-genre following a successful period elsewhere—you need to start reading. You've probably read this sub-genre or series romance line before, but there's a big difference between the way a reader reads and the way a writer reads. Don't put too much pressure on yourself about this. You may well find you don't have to *try* to read differently, you just naturally begin to observe a book in a new way. Some people like to take notes or analyse a particular line or sub-genre in a technical or academic way. If this works for you, great. If you'd rather learn by osmosis, do it that way.

Some of the things you'll want to look at are:

- Characters—do they tend to be warm and family-oriented? Edgy and in-your-face? Glamorous and sophisticated? Sassy and funny? Is the book closely focused on hero and heroine, or do the minor characters have strong roles and their own story arcs?
- Sex scenes—where do they fit on the steaminess scale?
- Settings—international or American? Big city or small town? Gritty or luxurious?

- Values—what kind of aspirations do the heroes and heroines have? What are they looking for? What kind of problems are they dealing with?
- Balance of content—are the books dominated by dialogue or by narrative? What is the balance between action and introspection? Do plot developments involve major drama, e.g. life-threatening danger, or day-to-day challenges like family arguments?
- Background and research—do the books treat the professions of the major characters as blurry wallpaper in the background, or are they integral to the story? Do the books offer readers a detailed and accurate window into a new world—say, the workings of a crime scene investigation team, or life on a Greek island—or are these settings covered in a few generic details?
- Pacing—are the books can't-put-down page-turners, or do they offer a more leisurely and nuanced reading experience?

Whichever method of analysis you're using, you'll eventually get a feel for the ingredients and boundaries in the area you've chosen. Some of these boundaries are easy to define—for example, many inspirational lines and imprints don't want consummated sex scenes outside of marriage. Others are more blurred. A certain line may be known for its wealthy, sophisticated heroes, but can this definition be pushed to include a self-made shipwreck hunter? A particular senior editor may not be a fan of exotic locations or blue-collar heroes, and this isn't necessarily obvious from your sampling of the books.

Be warned, also—boundaries move. You're at the mercy of changing editorial staff who may assess the market and decide on a shift in parameters without making any big announcement of the fact. Editorial taste and market dictates will always change over time. A series romance line long known for its cowboy heroes and ranch settings will phase these out if they stop selling well. Sex scenes that were considered edgy and envelope-pushing five years ago may seem tame in comparison with some of the stuff that's out there now.

In aiming your work at a certain area of the market, you need to keep on top of all this as much as you can, while recognising that if you're not in direct communication with an editor, it can be hard to learn their current thinking. The book you're reading now, even if it only came out this month, isn't an infallible guide. It represents what the editor wanted eighteen months or even two years ago, not necessarily what she wants now.

Some people seem to have a really sensitive ear to the ground when it comes to picking up on the next trend. They're the ones who made us want to read about kick-ass heroines when we thought we liked the girl-next-door, or for whom mere vampires weren't edgy enough, they had to be vampire shape-shifting homicide detectives. These writers may also be the people who had their first Blackberry when the rest of us still thought it was a fruit, and goodness knows what they're doing on the internet now, because some of us are still trying to work out what an RSS feed might be.

If, like me, you're not naturally one of these people—if you're positively tone-deaf when it comes to trends—then don't try to become one. You'll end up arriving at the party, dishevelled and out of breath, clutching your bottle of unfashionable wine, after everyone else has already left.

BOOK OF YOUR HEART

You have to play to your strengths, and if you're not trend-sensitive, then chances are you're sensitive to your own muse instead. What you need to focus on is writing the book of your heart.

At first glance this may seem impossible, given that you're attempting to fit into a set of boundaries or guidelines over which you have little control. If you're writing within a given series romance line, in particular, you're facing a challenge. In this case, what you'll be doing is writing a book of the heart by stealth, probably over the course of a number of different romance novels. You'll use one book to explore your feelings about a pregnancy loss, another to capture the joy you felt when you had your first baby at last, a third to deal with the realisation that your mother's declining health meant she couldn't play the role of devoted grandmother you'd imagined her in for so long.

Whether you're submitting to more than one line or imprint in the hope of getting published somewhere . . . anywhere, or whether you're already writing successfully for one segment of the market and are now branching out into a new one, you may experience a confusing split in your writing person-ality due to the differing requirements and expectations in your chosen areas. There are successful authors who write highly sensual love stories under one name and Christian, inspirational romance under another. There are authors whose readers will follow them from extravagant historical novels to edgy contemporaries and want more of both.

There are many ways to write in more than one area and make it work. Try taking a break between books when you're switching lines. Go back to reading—read the line or sub-genre you're about to write in if this works for you; if it doesn't work, read something completely different.

I like to send myself strong subliminal cues when I'm switching genres. For series romance, I'll write directly onto the computer, but for mainstream fiction I write my first drafts by hand. For series romance, I get straight into the story and research as I go along, while when I'm planning a mainstream book I'll do a ton of reading and thinking, make collages, cook regional food from where the book is set, and roam the internet for relevant sites before I put a word on the page.

Another way to keep the boundaries clear between your different writing fields is to consciously celebrate the strengths and possibilities within what you're currently writing. Instead of feeling frustrated that the line doesn't allow for much focus on secondary characters in a short series romance, celebrate the fact that you have more space to delve into your central relationship in satisfying detail.

Recognise the truth of the saying, 'A change is as good as a holiday'. After I'd been writing medical romances for some years, I added Silhouette Romance to my repertoire. Oh, how I loved the new opportunity to write about princesses, ranchers, millionaires and dress designers instead of doctors, nurses and paramedic teams! When I went back to a medical after writing a Silhouette Romance, my surgeons and paediatricians had a new freshness and zest thanks to my time away from them, and I relished the opportunity to deal with some more confronting emotional issues than the readers of Silhouette Romance wanted in their books.

MEETING READERS' NEEDS

Successful Silhouette Desire author Bronwyn Jameson has a very perceptive handle on why readers come back to a particular series romance line or romance sub-genre over and over again. They're not looking for the same *book*, they're looking for the same *reading experience*. It's all about how a book makes them *feel*, and they know how they want to feel. If they want to be scared, horrified, on the edge of their seat, shocked to their bones, kept on tenterhooks and ultimately rewarded with the knowledge of justice done and love winning through, they'll turn to romantic suspense or paranormal/fantasy. If they want to be touched, moved, warmed, made to smile one minute and cry the next, they may pick up a medical romance or contemporary women's fiction. If they want to laugh out loud and nod in wry recognition, they might read chick lit.

When you're writing within one of these sub-genres, you need to know how your readers want to feel and make sure you deliver on it with every book. It may take time to understand what readers love in your work. Is it really the hot sex, or is it the well-drawn characters and true-to-life emotional dilemmas? Is it your exotic tropical settings or would readers embrace your take on Wollongong, New South Wales or Boise, Idaho provided you gave them the same fast-paced plotting they've loved before?

If you look at the first of Janet Evanovich's Stephanie Plum novels, *One For The Money*, you'll find that it's edgier and darker than the later books. Reader response to this first book told her that what people loved was not the gritty violence and street-level crime but the New Jersey humour and the situational slapstick of Stephanie's somewhat careless approach to her bounty-hunting career. In subsequent books, Janet made sure she delivered, to keep readers coming back for more.

If you find you can't deliver anymore—you've done enough of *warm*, you really, really want to write *edgy*—then it's probably a sign that you need to add another line or sub-genre to what you're already writing, or target a different segment of the market if you're aiming to be published for the first time. Readers and editors may indeed want the same reading experience from you again and again, but they don't want it to be a tired one. You've probably read a book yourself from a long-time favourite author who only seems to be phoning in her performance this time around. You want to tell her to take a break or, if it's really bad, yell at her for not respecting her readers.

Switching sub-genres is something to think about very carefully, however. As a reader, you may have experienced picking up a new book by a once-loved author who's obviously grown restless and bored. Suddenly, instead of those believable ensemble pieces about women, love and family, she's thrown in a hokey murder plot and you're just not buying into the new direction. It's not that you wanted her to stay exactly the same through another thirty books, it's that she's not doing this new thing well enough.

WHERE DO YOU WANT TO GO?

When you switch sub-genres or add a new string to your romance-writing bow, you have to do it as well as you possibly can, and you have to think about it thoroughly. Ask yourself: Is this where I really want to go as a long-term future direction, or am I just feeling temporarily stale? Will I be able to write more books like this, or is it the only romantic suspense plot I'll ever come up with? Is there a different and better way to refresh my inspiration? Am I just jumping on the latest bandwagon? How do I signal to readers that this is a different kind of book? Should I use a new writing name, or is the new direction offering enough of what readers already love about me that they'll happily embrace what's different?

In answering these questions, look for feedback from someone who already knows and loves your writing—a critique partner, an agent or editor you respect, a supportive spouse, perhaps even some of your fans. Targeting a new section of the market means making a major creative investment. It may take months or years, as well as thousands of words written but never sold. Don't put in all that energy trying to reach a place you don't really want to be, or somewhere that doesn't suit who you are.

I would summarise what I've written here in three words—read, think, feel. Read widely across all romance lines and sub-genres to explore where you might fit. Think about it; it's not a casual decision, it's one that can determine the course of your entire career. Feel your way—trust your intuition, explore and trust your felt responses as a reader and as a writer. The market for romance in all its shifting forms is the candy store, and you are the kid with your eyes round with excitement and your pocket money in your hand. Celebrate your opportunities and your choices, and make them well.

LILIAN DARCY has written over seventy-five books for Silhouette Special Edition, Silhouette Romance and Harlequin Medical Romance in a career spanning more than twenty-five years. With this figure in mind, she wishes to claim that she sold her first book at age ten. Under another name she has also written for Australian theatre and television. Lilian's books have appeared numerous times on the Waldenbooks series romance weekly bestseller list and she is a three-time finalist in the Romance Writers of America's RITA Awards.

In 2008 Lilian celebrated the release of her first mainstream women's fiction novel, *Café du Jour* which the Melbourne *Age* called 'warm and witty . . . an excellent read'. She has presented workshops at the national conference of Romance Writers of America, and has taught romance writing at the University of Sydney's prestigious Centre for Continuing Education.

5

CODE READ:
Writing the modern medical

MEREDITH WEBBER

Modern medicals? Is that what I write? I hadn't much thought about the modern aspect, but yes, I guess the medical romance sub-genre has come a long way from the original doctor–nurse books. Although even back when the stories first became popular, the doctor and nurse were often serving in inhospitable places and were always caught up in the serious task of saving lives.

Medical romance involves its heroes and heroines in life-and-death situations, and while all medicals might not have breath-holding, fist-clenching, nail-biting scenarios, if that's what you want to write, then go for it. Medical romance is where such drama fits.

But so do hospital stories, country practice stories, flying doctor stories and emergency room stories—medical romances cover such a wide scope of medical and paramedical situations and settings that almost anything goes. Note the almost! As writers we write to meet reader expectations, and readers of medical romances are reading first and foremost for the romance. Readers want a hero with whom they can fall in love and a heroine to whom they can relate, and they want to see this couple's journey from that first tingle of attraction to their final declarations of love. They want to walk in the shoes of the hero and heroine as they battle through the odds to eventual happiness—that's the romance part. We add the medical to the romance first with a medical setting—some of which I've already mentioned—then by choosing a hero and heroine who are professionals in some medical or medically related field.

It is also important that they are working together. Why? you ask. Well, partly because it gives them the opportunity to get to know each other really well, to see how they each react in often stressful situations. It pushes them together when sometimes they don't want to be together, when they've had an argument, or when first they meet and they're not sure they even like each other. Oh, they're attracted to each other, our hero and heroine—that's a given—but attraction can be inconvenient, it can be unwanted, it can be uncomfortable, but it still tugs at the senses of the two people feeling it, teases at their minds, and nibbles at their nerve endings.

CREATING TENSION

Pushing your characters together creates tension—external tension—something that comes from outside, while inside them other tensions boil and seethe. She's been burned by love before, and doesn't trust it, doesn't need it, while he's seen the failed marriages of his parents, siblings and friends and knows it's not an institution intended for workaholics like him. Internal emotional tensions which involve the hero and heroine and are an obstacle to their relationship are vital, driving the development of the romantic relationship and the growth of the characters.

Tension in romances often goes under the name of conflict, and early on in your contemplation of a story, when the ideas chasing around in your head are giving off little threads of possibility, you need to be able to answer the question your editor is sure to ask: what's the conflict? What fear or anxiety is buried deep inside our hero and heroine that will make them determined to resist the attraction that has sparked between them? Think of a midwife with fertility issues who longs for a child of her own; marriages wrecked by the pressures of work but the couple reuniting; single dads struggling to cope—these are all popular emotional themes.

These are the things that attracted me to romance writing, but it was the research that brought me to writing medical romances. In the beginning, having no medical knowledge at all, I bought nursing and other medical books at Kmart when they had what they used to call 'brain-food' sales. And once I started to research, I was hooked, always finding something new to read about, some new discovery to wonder at and applaud. Reading a newspaper article about the Australian discovery of spray-on plastic skin led to a book with burns victims in it, a book that went on to be number one on the Waldenbooks bestseller list in the USA. For me every book is a new challenge, and the vast world of medicine ensures that the challenge stays fresh, because there is always something new to find out, and weave into my stories.

So, where to begin? I usually start with a situation that is going to put the characters into a particular setting. Although the characters are the most important part of the book, I don't feel ready to start writing until I know where the characters are going to be. My first book was largely set in India, a few books after that I used the setting of a temporary medical clinic high in the Himalayas—more of that later—and any number of my books have been set in the outback, or in busy emergency rooms. I've stuck my hero and heroine in refugee camps, one on a tropical island, one in the blistering heat and dust of the desert, and I've had them dropping out of helicopters into gorges, and battling disease in the aftermath of a cyclone. But you don't need adventurous settings for tension and excitement—imagine the tension of saving a child's life, or the thrill of delivering a baby.

SETTING AS CHARACTER

For me, the setting is like another character in the book, often the bad guy. One or both of my main characters will be new to the setting, and uncomfortable in it. Why? Because someone who is out of their normal environment is vulnerable, and a little vulnerability in a character makes him or her more appealing to the reader. It's true we're all drawn to super-confident people, but do we like them as much as we like those who show a little anxiety, or reveal a few cracks in the mask of confidence they wear? We can empathise with someone who has problems, even if it's something as minor as a heroine who has to wash her hair in bore water so goes around with her crowning glory smelling of rotten egg gas, and it is empathy with a character that draws a reader into the book, and makes him or her want to keep reading—if only to find a solution to the smelly hair problem!

Your setting can be anywhere that a couple of medical people might realistically be working. Realistically? Oh yes! Readers are savvy people and readers of medical romances often have medical backgrounds themselves, so you wouldn't 'realistically' have a first-class brain surgeon working out of a tiny country hospital, unless you can give a believable reason for his being there. Visiting his ageing mother when the car accident outside the town injures six teenagers? That would work, especially if one of the teenagers was the son of his old girlfriend—oh dear, I can feel a story coming on and that's not what I'm supposed to be doing right now. But as a writer, you can make the world you are creating work any way you like, providing you put in place reasons and motivations that are believable.

Writers are always striving to increase the level of tension in our books, and again, the setting can help to do that. It can provide an element of physical danger— from nature in the guise of snakes and crocodiles, or elemental danger like a cyclone, landslide or tidal wave (before we knew they were called tsunamis!). Then there's the danger inherent in war zones, in areas where landmines are still being cleared, or the danger of a hospital incident such as a drug-crazed madman loose in the ER. But as well as, and even more important than physical danger, the setting can provide emotional danger—or at least emotional challenges. The heroine from the outback who never, ever, *ever* wants to live there again—surely not the bore water/hair thing again!—sent out to work in a country hospital. She falls in love with the hero who is determined to stay there, so she has to face her past and come to terms with whatever it was that made her turn away from her birthplace—internal conflict, beautiful!

Or a hero who lost his wife and child in a car accident, now first on the scene at another accident, and having to rescue the child trapped in the car. Of course the paramedic who arrives is the woman he's attracted to—the first woman he's felt anything for since his wife died—so now he's reminded of the past, *and* feeling guilty for fancying our heroine, *and* trying to rescue the child, and the poor man is so tied up in knots the reader can't help but feel concerned for him and anxious to keep reading to see how he disentangles himself.

As professionals, our heroes and heroines will always cope—they'll do the jobs they have to do—but how much more powerful is the story when they are working to save lives while at the same time battling internal anguish and angst?

WHAT MAKES A HERO HEROIC?

Who are these wonder-people? Professionals, certainly, in a medical or medically related field, but they are more than that. Our heroes are heroic. Sounds simple, doesn't it, but it doesn't mean they have to abseil down cliffs to rescue the heroine—although they *would* do that—or throw themselves in front of a speeding train to save a dog. Our heroes are men we can look up to and admire, even aspire to be like—they are upright, decent, honourable men, whether they are the strong, silent type or the loudly demanding perfectionist, the bad boy made good, or the boy-next-door grown up, and all of them have a core of sensitivity that comes out when they sit beside a patient, listening or explaining, treating the person rather than the symptom or disease.

Where these superheroes hit trouble is when they fall in love. For a start, love can't be quantified or proven scientifically, so for a long time our hero has refused to believe it exists. When it does hit him, he's caught in a dilemma. If what he's feeling for the smart-mouthed paediatrician in Ward Five *is* love, what is he going to do about it? She's certainly not the person he imagined himself marrying. He's always wanted kids and isn't at all sure that Dr Smart-Mouth, who has undertaken years and years of study and risen to the top of her profession, would be willing to give it all up—or even give up a small amount of time—to have children.

If attraction is often inconvenient, then how much more unsettling is love? Of course, the joy of a romance rests in just that premise—that the strong, invulnerable male *can* be brought to his knees by an emotion too strong to go by any name but love.

But I've strayed away from the characters. We've looked at our heroes, so what about the heroines? In a 'modern' medical, our heroines are the heroes' equals— equally heroic, just as well qualified; women who can stand shoulder to shoulder with the hero in adversity, or fight him toe to toe over a difference of opinion. Our heroines can be everything a hero can be—rescue helicopter pilot, chief surgeon, fire-fighting paramedic, obstetrician, midwife—and more. More? Yes, more. Modern heroines are intelligent, savvy, well-educated women, but they retain the understanding, warmth and empathy good medical professionals need to make them great. For them, as for all women in this modern world, they might have to sacrifice family life—marriage and children—in order to pursue their studies, or to work in a high-pressure position, so their internal conflicts are often built in to their professional goals. *Can I give up all I've worked for to stay home and mind the children I know the man I love wants to have? Or can I have both?*

When I'm starting a new book, I begin with the situation or setting, then work out what characters will fit into it—or not fit into it if I want vulnerability. Having done that, for the next couple of weeks, while I pretend to do housework or other things, I'm actually living in my head, talking to my characters, getting to know them, seeing how they walk, hearing how they talk, catching snippets of conversation between them, garnering ideas for problems that might arise.

I'm totally unable to write a detailed plot of what is likely to happen in the book, so once I feel I know my characters sufficiently well to be able to tell their story, I sit down and write. I realise that it may sound daft to other people, but the impetus that keeps me writing down to the last full stop is to find out how the story finishes. Yes, I know I'm writing a romance, so I know my hero and heroine will get together at the end, but how are they going to overcome the problems between them? How will they get to that end? Finding the answers to these and other questions is what keeps me writing.

MEDICAL CONTENT

During the 'walking around in my head' weeks, I also do some research. Having decided on the medical or paramedical field in which my characters will be working, I check out what I need to know about it. The amount of medical detail in a modern medical romance varies from author to author and from book to book. You do need *some* medical details, and any you put in had better be right—I told you earlier, our readers are savvy!

While we don't need to describe in full detail the intricacies of brain surgery, we do need to draw our readers into the theatre while the operation is being performed, to feel the tension and drama of the event; or to have them feel as if they are sitting in a country doctor's office, where the pregnant teenager doesn't know how to tell her mum.

Medical content is as widely varied as medicine itself, and as far as I'm concerned, it depends on the book I'm writing at the time. I've recently done five linked books set in a large city hospital, in the unit where babies born with heart defects are operated on, sometimes as early as four days after birth. The more I researched the subject the more fascinated I became, and the more impressed I was by the dedication of the team of men and women who perform this type of surgery. The setting is made for drama, with trauma-tised parents struggling to understand the problems of their longed-for newborn, struggling to come to terms with the enormity of the operations he or she might face. Then there are the heart transplants—giving the heart of a dead baby to another baby so he or she might live. The trauma for one set of parents, the blessed relief of the other—how do professional people cope with this?

Into such a situation, you put a hero and heroine— maybe she's pregnant and aware every moment of every day that she's at work, that *her* child could have some problem. Or a couple whose marriage is rocky, wanting children but believing that one or other of them will have to give up work to care for the infants, reluctant to consider this because they believe all the training they have done would then be wasted. Would they be sacrificing the children they could save for selfish reasons? The issues are endless and the tension spirals tighter and tighter as the battle to save a baby's life becomes more and more desperate.

But whatever the medical situation, and however tense the medical drama, the focus must always remain on the hero and heroine. How are they handling it? How is it impacting on their very new and fragile relationship? Will it bring them closer or push them apart? Remember always that you are writing a romance, so every scene must affect the journey the hero and heroine take towards their mutual declaration of love. As the tension of the medical drama builds so must the tension of the emotional drama being played out alongside it. The purpose of the medical drama is not only to provide excitement, but to help the reader learn more about the characters, and to help move the relationship forward.

By now you should have gathered that the setting and situation are important, which is where I come back to my book set in the Himalayas. Somewhere I read about the medical outposts set up by the Himalayan Rescue Association during the trekking season along the routes most commonly used by tourists and touring parties. I was surprised to learn that although the staffing was on a volunteer basis, they had a two-year waiting list of doctors wanting to work in these clinics. I corresponded with the association and learned more, and was sufficiently fascinated by the idea to set a book there.

Big mistake. Oh, it was a good book—I thought a really good book—and my editor had liked it, but I had forgotten one key element. Readers like the familiar. When reading, they put themselves in the hero's or heroine's place and live the book through the characters. So it follows that they are more comfortable in surroundings they know—a city, a country town, even the Australian outback, which has been filmed and photographed enough for readers all over the world to feel they know it. But the Himalayas were foreign territory—too foreign, I feel, for many of my readers. And although my first book had been largely set in India, the journey of the hero and heroine had started and ended in Australia, not on the side of a steep mountain in Nepal.

KEEP IT UPBEAT

There is one more word that should get a mention here, and that is the word 'upbeat'. Although in the real world children die, and people don't get saved from plane crashes, it is important that your romance isn't dragged down by too much doom and gloom. Yes, a child might die in your book, but the child's death has to have good outcomes somewhere for the family—an end to suffering?—and also for the hero and heroine. It might draw them temporarily closer, or solve some tension between them, or cause more tension, but it mustn't ever just be there to fill the pages, or to bring a tear to the reader's eye. There will be lows in the book, but they only make the highs more joyous, and the culmination of the love story more emotionally satisfying. Remember—upbeat!

For me, writing medical romances is so exciting and fulfilling that I would encourage everyone with writing aspirations to give it a try. Like all writers of contemporary series romance, I am constantly asked whether I would like to write something else, and believe me, there are a few mysteries rattling around in my head, but recently I realised that I truly love what I do, and my ambition is to write better and better medical romances—maybe even a hundred of them! It's never too late to start and never too early to begin to hone your writing skills. And if you enjoy any of the medical serials on television, then maybe you'll enjoy writing similar stories, pitting your hero and heroine against death and disease, pushing them into dramatic situations where the growing attraction between them is tested. Just keep in mind that, first and foremost, you are writing a romance, and show the reader the love blooming between the hero and heroine, a love the reader can believe will last forever.

People working in medical and medically related fields *are* heroes and heroines, so you have ready-made characters to work with from the start. Just pluck them out of real life, put them in your book—fictionalised, of course—and let them come to life on the page, for you and for all the millions of readers who love and are inspired by modern medical romances.

MEREDITH WEBBER came late to romance writing, but soon became hooked and now has what she considers a perfect life. Through the hot months of summer she happily spends her time in the office, tapping away at the computer, while in cooler months she can be found way out west in the red desert country that she loves, grubbing away in the dirt in search of bright opals. With seventy-five published books to her credit, she is hoping this idyllic life will continue until she reaches a hundred—either in books or years, she's not fussy.

6

TONS OF ROMANCE
in the Regency

ELIZABETH ROLLS

If you are already writing historical romantic fiction, either published or unpublished, and believe that *for your writing* historical accuracy isn't an issue, beyond not having your Regency heroine in a miniskirt and halter-neck top, then read no further. Skip to the next chapter at once.

Likewise, if you're after detail on what your Regency heroine might have been gossiping about, reading or wearing in 1813, you're not going to find it here.

This chapter is my take on why research is fun and how to make it not only relevant, but vital to your story. This is about concepts and ideas, not detail. Although

I use Regency examples, the principles can be applied to any period.

Why write a Regency, or any historical novel? In fact, why write?

The answer for me comes down to the voices in my head trying to get out. You probably have them too. People with voices in their heads are either writers or clinically insane. Possibly both.

But what makes these 'people' in our heads what they are? What gives them the strength to force their way beyond daydreams onto the page?

It's going to be different for all of us, but for me, I've always loved history. I'm fascinated by stories about people who lived long ago in what felt like another world. My earliest recollection of this is a Ladybird book on William the Conqueror. I was absolutely shocked at age five to read that Earl Harold broke a solemn promise—sworn on *holy relics*, whatever they were. I said as much to my father, who snorted and told me Duke William was an opportunistic thug with no right to the English throne, and that Earl Harold was defending his country. It was my first taste of conflicting interpretations in the historical arena.

So I grew up loving stories with historical settings: Jean Plaidy's novels; Hilda Lewis's *The Gentle Falcon*; Geoffrey Trease's stories—*Cue for Treason* is a cracker. Finally, in my early teens, I connected with Georgette Heyer and Jane Austen. But it wasn't until my thirties that one of the stories in my head broke out. This was due to a difficult work situation and missing the whole writing process after finishing my thesis. Escape was needed and reading wasn't quite cutting it. So the story that became *The Unexpected Bride* was born and its characters and setting were unmistakably Regency.

Like seems to beget like and I've kept on writing Regencies. The more I find out the more fascinated I become. Luckily for me the market wants Regencies, but I am constantly aware of an itch to write stories in other periods. Other periods don't sell as well, but that isn't going to stop me. It's important to stay fresh and to keep learning, and I see researching a different period as a way to keep my stories fresh. You may have a different way of staying fresh.

So, we have these people in our heads and a story unfolding around them. And yes, unquestionably the story is the important thing. We pick up a novel for the story first and foremost. If the story doesn't engage us no amount of beautiful description or accurate history will make up for it. But people don't live in a vacuum, their stories happen within time and space, so as writers we have to build a world capable of sustaining these people, giving them life, giving them hell on the journey and, ultimately, love.

Another way to think about your choice of fictional world is to imagine someone with a glorious singing voice. Put the singer outdoors, and that glorious voice won't travel very far. In a vacuum it won't travel at all. But bring the voice inside, put it in a perfectly designed and built space, and it will resonate to fill the space and touch all listeners. The voice is the important thing, not the building. The listeners might not even notice the space, but without it the voice is lost. Just as the space enhances and focuses the voice, your setting should enhance and give form to your story. We have to build a consistent, believable world for our characters. I think the reason a television series like *Fawlty Towers* works so brilliantly, apart from terrific acting and script writing, is that the tightly knit setting provides a focus to heighten the comedy.

But what sort of world should we build? To research or not to research? Not everybody wants to research. Plenty of readers and writers alike consider the story, the romance, is enough. As a writer, I like to research. It's part of my process. Most of my ideas are sparked by things I've read. Something catches my imagination, and suddenly I have a 'What if—?'. I'm not saying that one way of writing is 'right' and any other way is 'wrong'. We all have to find our own process and for me the research is part of it. What I find out sparks ideas for plots and illuminates character.

The spark for my book *His Lady Mistress* was reading about the laws on suicide in the early nineteenth century; if the coroner brought in a verdict of suicide without the softener of 'while being of unsound mind', you were buried at a crossroads with a stake through your heart and all your property was sequestered. Your fifteen-year-old daughter was left destitute? Tough. This gave me a path into Verity Scott's story.

Too often there is an attitude that we can't have both accurate history and a good story. That too much history will 'slow the book down' or 'make it boring'. Badly used history, no matter how accurate, will certainly do both. We shouldn't 'info dump' history any more than we should 'info dump' a character's back story—the term 'info dump' being shorthand for sharing all your research with the reader right up front. (Historical romance author Jo Beverley includes historical notes at the end of her books to deal with that temptation.) But that doesn't mean that we can't make our settings accurate as well as entertaining.

For me, the more strongly we can build our characters' world, the more we know about that world, the stronger the story will be. Robert McKee puts it like this: 'There is no such thing as a portable story. An honest story is at home in one, and only one, place and time.' (See further reading at end of chapter.)

The trick is to recognise what *we* need to know, as opposed to what *the reader* needs to know. Sometimes we just need to know something in order not to create something anachronistic. Usually the reader doesn't need all the details of how to strike a spark from a tinderbox, but we need to know about tinderboxes so our heroine doesn't use a match. In *His Lady Mistress* my heroine had to use a tinderbox when she was very upset. I realised that the fiddly process would be difficult when she was crying and her hands were shaking, so I described the process in relation to how hard she was finding it. I used the detail to *show* her emotional state over her father's death, rather than writing 'Verity was terribly upset'. We need to know the marriage laws not to write a treatise on them, but to make sure our hero and heroine's marriage is legally valid, and possibly to create conflict.

But why bother, when there are plenty of readers out there who neither know nor care about these things?

Believe me, there are plenty of readers who know and care very much, especially when you're writing a Regency. But apart from that, *we* care. (Remember, I warned you to skip this chapter if necessary.) We want to write the best book we can. We want to give our characters hell. We want to throw as many seemingly insurmountable obstacles in their path as possible. Obstacles that would make less heroic mortals decide that this love thing isn't worth the trouble. So when they do triumph, they triumph gloriously. That way we know their happy-ever-after ending will stick.

The more real your conflict, the more strongly you can root your story in the soil of the Regency or any other historical period, including the present, the better it will flower. The more you know, the more options you have and the easier it is to avoid clichés. What would be the point of setting your story in a hospital unless the hospital setting was somehow vital to the story?

For an example, let's have a look at those marriage laws, and a real-life scenario—the Berkeley inheritance scandal.

Very briefly, Frederick Augustus, Fifth Earl of Berkeley, fell in love with Mary Cole, the daughter of a Gloucestershire tradesman. They married *officially* in 1796, by which time there were two sons. Can you see where this is going? In 1801 Frederick Augustus claimed that they had been married *privately* in 1785, but when he died this could not be proved to the satisfaction of the courts. The eldest son, William, inherited the castle by his father's direct bequest, but he could not inherit the title because by law that had to go to Thomas, the first son born after the 1796 marriage. As far as the law of inheritance was concerned Thomas was the oldest *legitimate* heir, and there was absolutely no way around that for any of them. The inheritance laws, particularly as they touched on titles and entailed property, were brutal. If a marriage could not be proved, or could be proved invalid, the children of that marriage were rendered illegitimate, and cut out of the succession. In fact, a child born out of wedlock was considered *filius nullius*, or child of no one. Legitimate children had rights of inheritance, illegitimate children had none unless specifically named in a will. One assumes the Fifth Earl realised that William was very likely to be barred from the title and worded his will accordingly.

Now, let's look at this as the scenario for a story.

If we were telling a story based on the original couple in this scenario, we want them to have a happy future. Marrying a tradesman's daughter where it wasn't a matter of saving the family fortunes was a shocking thing for our aristocratic hero. So there's his internal conflict—love versus family and social expectation. And it wasn't just snobbery. Who you married was important in terms of socio-political power. Marriage was seen as a social contract involving money and property; love ran a very poor second and was often seen as downright dangerous. Marrying a woman with property could bring more parliamentary seats under your control. Marrying a woman with a large monetary dowry meant you could provide for younger sons and daughters while maintaining and increasing your wealth to pass on to your heir. This maintained the family's socio-political position. That was how the system worked—but our hero wants love.

Perhaps our hero considers making the heroine his mistress. She might refuse, and/or he might realise what a cad he's being. The next step up would be to marry her, but keep the marriage secret. Having his cake and eating it. Only look what a mess that could get everyone into.

In the end our hero, being truly heroic, doesn't sneak around trying to hide his marriage and being ashamed of his bride. He might have to do some soul searching, but in the end he marries her proudly and publicly and makes damn sure his heir *is* his heir and that his wife is not subjected to gossip and social ostracism. Nor does he leave a shocking legal and emotional disaster for his sons to disentangle. (In the real-life case, neither William nor Thomas married at all.)

This is a different story, but it's all sprung from that snippet of knowledge about the Berkeley case. There are all sorts of things you can add to create external conflict—her father, trying to stop his only child being tricked by an aristocrat; his mother, trying to arrange an eligible match for him with a duke's daughter—and all sorts of complications and details to make the conflict real and true. Knowing the social history will broaden your range of possibilities, helping you to avoid the dreaded cliché.

Let's look at it another way. Let's tell the story of one or both of the sons of this union. What if Papa *did* contract a secret marriage? And what if he did later make the marriage public and even go through a second ceremony? And what if doubt arose about the truth of that supposed first marriage? What if at the end of the day that first marriage couldn't be proved? How will this affect the older brother? Has he married? Does he have children? How will this affect his marriage?

Or is he about to marry? Will this test the truth of his betrothed's affections? Or save him from a miserable marriage? What about the younger brother? Does he want this? Has he pushed the issue? Or is he standing back, as the real Thomas did, to avoid publicly shaming his mother? And what about any daughters? How does this affect their chances of marriage if they were proved to be illegitimate? The answer would be: badly. Illegitimacy wasn't just a minor embarrassment, it was a very real social and legal disaster for anyone born outside wedlock.

This is real conflict, based solidly on the laws of the period. It's still your story. Getting the history right will only strengthen it because there are no easy outs for anyone. Either brother can be your hero, and it's up to you if he ends up being Earl of All-He-Surveys, or just gets the girl. He's a hero so he'll be happy whichever way it turns out. In fact, Julia Quinn's *The Lost Duke of Wyndham* and the companion book, *Mr Cavendish, I Presume*, turn on a very similar premise but without the spectre of illegitimacy.

The Berkeley case is a specific example, using verifiable historical facts to spark ideas for a story. What about the more subtle aspects of the Regency? All those double standards about sex. Society turning a blind eye towards a man with a stable of previous and current mistresses (rake) and a woman with a past (slut, whore, fallen woman). These attitudes are still with us so they resonate with modern readers. In the Regency they were compounded by the fact that once a woman was married and had produced the requisite 'heir and a spare' she was often free to do as she pleased as long as she was discreet. The eleventh commandment: Thou Shalt Not Get Found Out. Many husbands were complacent. Of course many were not. You can use that too.

For an unmarried girl it was another matter. She was supposed to be handed over to her husband *virgo intacta* so he had a fighting chance of knowing that his heir was indeed his son. So an unmarried girl agreeing to sex is taking one almighty risk. She is risking her own chance of marriage and security. She is risking utter social and financial ruin. Actually, she was taking a hell of a risk with her reputation just being alone with a man, let alone going to bed with him. Don't let that get in the way of your story though. Acknowledge her risk, use it, and you've immediately raised the stakes. Think of the fate of Maria in Jane Austen's *Mansfield Park*—and she was lucky. Look at Thomas Hardy's *Tess of the d'Urbervilles*—set much later and it has a tragic ending, but it gives you a very clear idea of the ostracism a 'fallen woman' might face. The more you know about the taboos and shibboleths of any period, the more powerfully you can use them.

If you want a heroine versed in the radical writings of Mary Wollstonecraft, make sure she is the sort of woman who would have read them. Make sure she *acts* like the sort of woman who would read something that provocative. Wollstonecraft's writings were revolutionary in the true sense of the word. They were considered, quite literally, dangerous in a climate where the government was terrified of new ideas sparking a revolution à la the French model. A woman who reads them is unlikely to be a gently reared, conventional young lady. On the other hand, she will certainly give the hero hell and make him question his sanity in falling in love with her—all of which is only going to enhance your story.

If you do create a heroine who thinks differently to most of her counterparts, make sure that you set that against what was normal for the period and use it to create tension and up the stakes.

And speaking of the French Revolution, what about the Napoleonic Wars? You at least need to know that they happened, or were happening, depending on the exact date of your story. You could hardly set a story in June 1815 without some reference to Waterloo, for example. In fact, if you didn't want to deal with Waterloo, that would be a good reason for picking another date. If you do have a bent towards military history then the Napoleonic Wars are an absolute goldmine for conflicted characters and situations. But if you are going to dip your toe in here, get the facts right as far as possible. The history will not ruin your story, only enhance it.

But, I hear you wail, *I don't* want *to worry about wars and marriage laws! I want to write a nice, light-hearted romp! A social comedy, not high drama.*

That's fine too. But we need to understand the context of that social comedy, or how can we make it truly entertaining? How can we point up the foolishness or irony of something we don't quite understand? Consider *Fawlty Towers* again. The subject matter is human nature in all its idiotic glory. Because the writers set up a very tight, consistent setting, Basil and Sybil et al. are constantly driven to *extremis* by its constraints. Understanding the social setting focuses the comedy.

So, your heroine is going to London for the Season. Her motive is to make a Good Marriage, by which she means A Title. Or at least Money. Preferably Old Money. But why? Sheer snobbery? That's hardly an attractive motive, is it?

But look at the political and social motivation underlying the London Season. The Season happened because that was when Parliament was in session. The peerage was in London not because they wanted to party, but to carry out their political responsibilities. A side effect of this, though, was that it was a very good time to make sure a girl met as many eligible men as possible. Not all girls were given a Season, however. Giving a girl a Season was very expensive and families who could afford it looked upon it as an investment. If you spent all that money and effort on your daughter you expected her to oblige you and marry someone who would add to your family's power base and prestige. A girl who chose to buck this system and marry only for love was not going to endear herself to her family. Of course your heroine can marry a poor man for love— just don't expect her family to be delighted about it.

Likewise, even a very wealthy man had to take into account the fact that he was expected to hand on his wealth and property to his heir. His bride's dowry was meant to contribute to providing for younger sons and dowries for his daughters. If he died, his widow would be entitled to a third of the estate income for her life unless she remarried. He had to provide for that. Just imagine if not only his mother but also his grandmother were still living and the estate was providing for them. He needs a very wealthy bride. So what does he do? I can see at least two ways to give him hell here. I could force him to marry the daughter of a merchant for her money, or have him accidentally compromise a girl from an impoverished family so that he ends up having to marry *her*.

Either way he has a major marital problem with no exit sign. He either has to convince the merchant's daughter that he really does love her and that her money doesn't matter in the end, or he has to convince the other girl that he doesn't regret their marriage and that he will find a way to turn his family fortunes around anyway. And if he was about to become betrothed to the merchant's daughter at the start of the book before compromising the second girl, so much the better.

The thing is, you have to understand *why* he needs that wealthy bride to make his conflict strong enough. He has to love his family and want to do the right thing by them. He might even like the merchant's daughter and feel terrible about having to back out of the planned betrothal because he knows that this will damage her reputation. But what else can he do when a child's prank left him locked in a cellar all night with the other girl and tongues are wagging? (Okay, that's a really clichéd device, but with a little bit of research I could do much better.) And let's face it, I can give the merchant's daughter her happy-ever-after in the next book and everyone will be happy, including my editor.

Using history to strengthen your story is not just a matter of researching what clothes your characters would have worn to a party; it's far more complex. Also, if you need to know what clothes your heroine is wearing, make sure you understand how they were worn and with what undergarments. Then, if your hero decides to strip your heroine naked after the party, you know exactly what he's doing and how much fun they're having while he's doing it. Using history is about giving your story a frame and background to support its structure. Using history is about enhancing the story, not giving the reader a history lesson. And let's face it, history *has* 'story' right there in the word. It's up to us to squeeze it out.

The same principle applies as if you were writing a contemporary novel; use background and detail if it is going to illuminate character, drive the plot, or create change. If your Regency heroine goes on a shopping spree, don't make it an occasion to show how much you know about Regency fashion in 1816. Use it to show something about your heroine. Perhaps she has always been a country mouse. Perhaps she is shy and has always chosen inconspicuous clothing. Don't take us shopping with her just to give her (and us) more of the same. Change her. Make her change of wardrobe reflect her inner change. And use your knowledge of what she chooses to make it real and vital.

Researching dress is relatively easy; there's plenty to start with on the internet, and a few questions to other writers will bring up a slew of books. A wonderful starting place on the internet is the links page on author Anne Gracie's website (www.annegracie.com). She lists any number of useful sites on fashion and other research tidbits.

Every writer approaches research differently. Some things—details of dress, food, the small stuff—I check out as I go. There's not much point in researching in minute detail every aspect of my heroine's dress before writing. For me that's an excuse to delay writing. If you find that you need to know what your heroine wears before she'll even speak to you, go right ahead. It's your process.

On the other hand, if my heroine was going to travel from, say, Yorkshire to London as part of the plot, and important things were going to happen to her on the way, I'd research the route and her method of travel first. Then I'd know where she went, and if I needed somewhere convenient for her to be kidnapped I'd have a better idea of where to set up the ambush. What I find out may well give me ideas and shape events.

Use travel details if you are writing a road-trip story. Otherwise readers don't need travel details beyond how long the trip took. They need to know that she got there and took roughly the right amount of time to do it. This is why I give very few travel details in *A Compromised Lady*. The story opens in Yorkshire, but most of it happens in London, so my heroine Thea only had to get from Yorkshire to London. It wasn't a road story. Nothing happened on that journey except she read, talked to her brother, played chess with him and a horse lost a shoe. None of which is mentioned in the book because they didn't affect the story.

The trick is to know when to use detail of setting and period, and when not to. You don't need to describe every item of furniture in a room, unless your point-of-view character has a very good reason for noticing what's there. On the other hand, *you* may need to know what's there so that if you have another scene in that room later you don't put the desk on top of the sofa or have the windows on an inside wall. I find the easiest method here is to find a picture of the right sort of room and just move in (metaphorically speaking). There are some fabulous books available on period interiors. Two that I find helpful are *Eighteenth-Century Decoration: Design, and the Domestic Interior in England* by Charles Saumarez Smith (Weidenfeld & Nicolson, 1993) and *Authentic Décor: The Domestic Interior 1620–1920* by Peter Thornton (Weidenfeld & Nicolson, 1993).

You also need to be prepared to think of ways of explaining some historical custom or fact that may not be apparent to a reader without turning it into a history lesson. Or you may need to modify a historical term to avoid giving your readers the wrong idea. When Meg, the heroine of *The Dutiful Rake*, was ill, she had to use an invalid's cup with a spout. This was known as a 'sick syphon'. My editor asked if I could call it something less likely to turn the readers off, so we compromised with a 'sickroom syphon'. It's a balancing act between anachronism and remembering that you are writing for today's and tomorrow's readers.

For me the story is definitely the propelling force. My characters are paramount. I want them to live and breathe so that my readers can relate to them. Emotion does not change from one generation to another. But how those emotions are expressed will change. Social expectations will change. Ways of doing things will change, from the simple, like cleaning a gown, to the complex, like how the marriage laws worked.

And always, *always* there are things we need to know simply to avoid putting in or implying something that could not have happened. It's like the old saw, 'You need to know what you don't know, in order to know what you don't need to know'. Don't expect to find out everything before you start writing. You will most likely make mistakes. Just keep reading and learning and they won't be the same mistakes.

If you can start to get a handle on the issues and details that affect your characters' lives, even if you don't use the detail in the story, you stand a better chance of getting right into your characters' skins, and beneath the surface of your story. And that's what it's all about, whether you write a historical or a contemporary romance—understanding what makes your characters tick. Knowing where, when and how they lived is just as important as knowing their favourite colour and the name of their pet dog. We are all products of time and place; why would our characters be any different?

FURTHER READING

Story: Substance, Structure, Style and the Principles of Screenwriting by Robert McKee (Methuen, 1999).

Berkeley Castle by Vita Sackville-West (Heritage House Group, 2004).

Multi-award-winning author ELIZABETH ROLLS lives in the Adelaide Hills of South Australia with her husband and two sons. She shares her desk with the cat and the rest of the office with three dogs. So far the fences are keeping the sheep and alpacas at bay. She has finally realised that the best way to deal with anyone asking how she 'researches' a love scene is with the answer: 'The same way I'd research a murder scene.' More information about Elizabeth and her books can be found at www.elizabethrolls.com.

7

TWO WORLDS:
Weaving romance with fantasy

KELLY ETHAN

Like any good story, a fantasy romance has to have a strong plot. Given most fantasy romances, in particular epic fantasies, tend to be of a much longer word count than traditional romances, usually in the 100 000-word range, the plot must be strong enough to carry the story right to the end. The first thing I do is come up with an idea. It might be sparked by a magazine article about nanotechnology or DNA. Or something I see on television. Some little thing that ignites my imagination and gets me excited.

Once I have that spark, the story starts to fall into place in my mind and then it's time to decide what sub-genre of fantasy my story will fit into. When I wrote

The Beast Within, the plot very quickly dictated that this story would be an urban fantasy. This is the cover blurb for *The Beast Within*:

What's a girl to do when she can't change into the family wolf and Mr. Beast kidnaps her man? Take the evil on and kick some ass—with or without a furry coat.

Cassidy Quinn, Private Investigator extraordinaire, helps down and dirty humans and monsters of Memorial City . . . for a price. But when a friend phones with a puzzling medical case, Cassidy knows the big bad has come to town—in the form of a rogue werewolf out for blood. Making herself known to the new evil, she fights against his web of deceit and lies, battling to save her friends, family and sexy police detective Patrick Logan. One problem—the beast has targeted Cassidy for his mate and he has the upper fang since she's stuck in human form. When Cassidy finds Logan all too seductive a distraction, the beast's anger explodes and Logan is kidnapped by the werewolf. Can Cassidy find Logan before it's too late and he becomes the main course?

I'm often asked where I get my ideas. I use my imagination. How about taking an idea from history and adding in a smidgeon of alien infestation, or a wizard? Maybe an elf or two? The sky's the limit. In fantasy romance, anything is possible as long as you are consistent and the actions of your characters match the world in which you set your story. What you can't do is take a standard romance plot and throw in a few fantasy elements. The fantasy has to be integral to the plot, as does the romance. The tighter you interweave the two, the better your story.

Once you've decided where your story is set, and have your plot outlined, it's time to think about your main characters. You want to hook your reader into your world so you have to make it believable. Or so exciting and interesting they are willing to suspend disbelief and live in your world for a while. This calls for strong, three-dimensional characters who come alive on the page. Whatever your character does, make it fit in with his or her world, not stand out as something that happens in ours. Unless, of course, you're setting your fantasy in the contemporary world. Then there is a whole new set of rules to contend with.

Don't make your characters so alien your reader can't identify with them. Regardless of their species, give them foibles that the reader can relate to. I like to give my characters quirks. In *The Beast Within*, my werewolf character liked to chew her one claw that pops out when she's worried. It's something that every nail-biter can relate to, and makes the character less than perfect.

Names are important too. They must suit the setting, the world you've created. In a medieval fantasy, whoever heard of characters called Bunny or Missy? Make the names, clothing and architecture suit the time period you're using.

Readers tell me they dislike names or punctuation they find hard to pronounce. Some of the many naming sites on the internet will help you when it comes to christening your characters. Here are a few I've used:

www.kabalarians.com/cfm/menu-briefanalysis.cfm
rinkworks.com/namegen/
www.gaminggeeks.org/Resources/KateMonk/
And just for fun, name your pet:
www.bowwow.com.au/search/index.asp

Be careful when using modern settings. In some ways they are easier because you don't have to build the whole world from scratch, but you'll need to be far more accurate and observant of the rules of everyday life than you do if you build your own world. If you choose an actual town that exists in this time, you can guarantee at least one of your readers will know that town intimately. Get it right or you'll hear from that reader.

Every author constructs their story in their own way. Author Alexis Fleming, who also happens to be my mother, says she came up with the setting and plot for her fantasy romance *Emerald Ice* because she has always been fascinated by the unexplained events attributed to the Bermuda Triangle.

Alexis says, 'I was determined to one day write a story set in this area. The ideas bubbled around in my head for ages before I finally settled on a plot. *Emerald Ice* is the story of an ancient race of alien colonists who settled on an island hidden in the middle of the Bermuda Triangle, where they mined an alternative fuel source from the core of the planet, a source of energy that the governments of Earth knew nothing about.

'My heroine, Tia, has been raised as human and taught to suppress all emotion, but one flash of temper transports her to the island where she finds out she's the Oracle of the Alterran people. Before she knows it, she's caught in a political struggle and is helping the hero, Lord Connor, take his rightful place as ruler of his people.'

According to Alexis, hers is a story of good versus evil, of magical powers, and a passionate romance that will change the face of the alien culture. 'I knew my setting from the word go, and although this is set in contemporary times, I knew I needed to make the alien culture different enough to be believable. What I did was take a moment in history and bend it to fit my story. I set the alien society up to follow the main traits of ancient Roman life, with the magic and alien powers thrown in, but with far superior technology.

'I was lucky enough to connect up with one of the writers for *Star Trek: Voyager*, who helped me work on the ore the aliens were mining and set it securely within the rules of physics. This gave the whole story believability and I'll be forever grateful to that man. And who knows? Maybe aliens are responsible for all the strange happenings in the Bermuda Triangle.'

If you choose to use magic as the basis of your plot, remember there are rules to follow. You have to establish those rules so your reader understands them. Don't use your magic as a crutch. If your hero knows that he can solve all problems with the flick of a wrist, where's the suspense? There must be a price to be paid for the use of magic. Is there a physical weakness if your hero uses his magic? Does his health suffer? Does he need time before his magic is at full strength again? All actions have consequences and that applies to the use of magic. Make your rules and then adhere to them consistently.

WORLD-BUILDING

The type of world you build depends on the type of romantic fantasy you're writing. In *The Beast Within*, the world was an *open* urban fantasy: the werewolves and other supernaturals had 'come out' fifty years before my story started. I had the normal modern world already made for me and I just added a dash of the supernatural. I still had to build rules for the supernatural elements within the realistic world, but for all intents and purposes, the framework for my story and the world it was based in were already set up.

For my second novel, *Miss Predictable*, I again chose the urban, modern world, but this time I set up a *closed* world. The main characters in this book were Greek gods who had moved Mount Olympus, the home of the gods, to a casino in Las Vegas. They were hiding in plain sight. They had their own subculture within Las Vegas, but no one in the human world realised. Hence the closed-world tag, the magical or supernatural world hidden away from others. Here is the cover blurb for *Miss Predictable*:

What does a girl do when she's surrounded by Greek God wannabes and someone's out for her blood? Find herself a hunky Greek God and have great sex . . . er, fall in love, of course.

Cassandra Troy comes from a long line of fortune tellers and her mother is no exception. Having sworn off the business, when her mother goes missing she's not impressed, and has to track her down before the family business drives her round the twist. But with strange accidents, an inability to tell a lie, a hunky hotel manager named Hermes and a host of family members who swear they're Greek Gods of mythology, the task might be harder than she thought. It's time for a girl to lay down the law.

Can Cassandra stop a vengeful lover, and save her well-meaning mother and her sexy God Hermes in time?

Once you've set up the rules for your world, make certain your characters remain true to those rules. Your reader has to believe in your world and relate to what your characters are going through.

Start by defining your physical world. Sometimes it helps to draw a map of the various geological features. If your story is set in a town or city, draw a map of the streets, mark where the hero lives, and so on. It all helps when it comes to writing your story.

There are many elements to take into account in world-building. What is the landscape like? The flora and fauna? What are the buildings made of? What is the culture like? Here are some of the elements I focus on:

- geography
- plants that grow in your world
- animals living there
- the air they breathe
- the food they eat
- clothing
- monetary units
- social and cultural mores

- units of measure
- politics
- what the buildings look like
- schooling
- the military and the weapons they use
- language.

You may not use all these elements in your story, but you have to know them well enough to make your story seamless and believable for the reader. You have to keep track of every nuance of society. The devil is in the detail. The more you develop your world, the more comfortable you'll be in it, and the more real it will seem to your reader.

If you do an internet search on world-building, you'll find stacks of information available. Here's one site to get you started: www.sfwa.org/writing/worldbuilding1.htm.

No writing is easy, but writing fantasy romance is probably one of the more difficult genres. There's so much to keep track of. You can't afford to drop the ball even once because your readers will surely spot the mistakes. It's also a competitive market to break into so you need to be determined.

Despite the challenges, writing fantasy of any description is a whole lot of fun. Creating a brand-new world. Burying yourself in an era long gone. Meeting the characters who people your world. Yes, there's the challenge, but there's joy in the accomplishment—crafting a fantasy romance that sweeps your readers away to a whole new, exciting reality.

It's been said that every novel ever written is a fantasy and, technically, that's true if you consider that the events in the story never actually happened. One of the first things I learned was the difference between romantic fantasy and fantasy romance.

Romantic fantasy is a sub-genre of fantasy. It's set in a fantastical world and concerns the development of the social, political and romantic relationships of the characters. Okay, so far it sounds like my version of a fantasy romance, but here's where I came unstuck. In a romantic fantasy, although the romance may be a key component of the story, the plot, characterisation and world-building are more important. These are character-driven rather than romance-driven plots, and don't always have the happily-ever-after of a romance story.

A fantasy romance is a different beast. Yes, it still follows the rules of a fantasy novel, but it mixes in elements from the fantasy and the romance genre, appealing to readers from both fields.

WHAT IS FANTASY?

My definitions have been garnered through extensive reading and research of the fantasy genre. Other writers may have different concepts. I see fantasies as stories set around fantastical elements such as magic and other supernatural happenings. They form an intrinsic part of the plot and theme of the story. The story can be set in a totally fictitious and imaginative world you've created, or it can be set firmly in this world, as you'll see when we examine the many sub-genres fantasy romance has spawned. Fantasy stories differ from science fiction in that they avoid the more high-tech, science-based machinery and ideals.

We hear that there are only so many plots, that it's all in how the author presents the story. Fantasy uses plot devices which are standard fare for this type of story. Good versus evil. Fairy tales and legends. Magical objects. The quest. Magic in all its forms. Mythology and folklores. Medievalism. Sentient races. Dragons. Aliens.

If you're stuck for an idea, take one of these plot devices and play with it. It won't be long before your brain bubbles over with possibilities. You're limited only by your imagination, although having made your choices, they will limit what your characters can get up to in the story.

BLENDING ELEMENTS

As stated, fantasy romance is a blending of the elements of fantasy and romance writing. Fantasy romances weave together the fantasy elements of the magical and the paranormal with the ideals of a romance—a story centred around the developing relationship between two characters and the conflicts within that relationship. The two must run side by side. The central focus of a fantasy romance is the relationship between your main characters. This is not a fantasy with a romantic sub-plot.

The Beast Within is set in a contemporary world, but one where werewolves are commonplace. My heroine, Cassidy Quinn, is a werewolf who is also a private investigator. When a rogue werewolf comes to town, he steals a ritual text so he can perform a ceremony to divorce himself from the human aspects in his make-up. He decides to kill any human who knows he is connected with the text. Cassidy sets out to take the rogue down, even knowing that he wants her for his mate.

In the process, she meets Patrick Logan, a tough Irish cop who is investigating the murders. Logan is very alpha: strong, sarcastic, and more than ready to give Cassidy a run for her money. The two of them are thrown together constantly and sparks fly, despite Logan's suspicion that Cassidy is involved in the murders. And even if she isn't, damn it, he doesn't want her interfering in his case.

Although this is urban fantasy, the growing attraction and the sexual tension between these two drive the story forward. I had to keep the hunt for the killer going while focusing on the relationship between the hero and heroine. The suspense in the plot, combined with the fantastic world of the rogue werewolf, creates danger that increases the stakes and the tension between Cassidy and Logan, giving them an awareness of each other throughout the whole story. The fantasy elements and the world of lycanthropy provide a backdrop for the romance, until Cassidy and Logan reach their satisfying ending.

Which takes precedence, the fantasy or the romance? Neither. Ideally, if you take out either the fantasy or the romance, the story falls over. The fantasy elements enrich the romance and bring about a sense of drama. As with any romance, you must have the happily-ever-after ending to satisfy the reader. You want to submerge your reader in your rich fantasy world, so that they are willing to suspend disbelief and enjoy the journey of romantic discovery of your main characters.

Australian fantasy author Louise Cusack has given a lot of thought to what defines a fantasy romance as opposed to a fantasy that contains a romantic sub-plot. She says: 'The difference between "a fantasy romance", and "a fantasy novel that contains a romance" is simply your greater or lesser focus on the world-building (politics, magic, creatures etc.). Novels that sit on the Fantasy Shelves in bookstores are those that focus on world-building, and just happen to have a love story as part of the plot. To sit on the Romance Shelf, your novel has to be *all about the romance* and the world-building needs to be background to that—that's the definition of "a fantasy romance". Unfortunately, that doesn't mean you can get away with doing less work in developing your fantasy world, it just means that you show less of it to the reader because you're consistently focusing the reader's attention on the developing romance.'

A WORLD OF SUB-GENRES

So many sub-genres have grown out of the original traditions on which fantasy storytelling was based that it can be confusing at times. Although I don't have room to include all of the variations, the main sub-genres within the fantasy romance field at the time of writing are listed below.

Alternative history

Alternative history is generally set in a world that parallels ours, but with subtle changes in historical, social, political and industrial events. It's a big 'what if' story, such as: what would have happened if the Roman Empire still existed? If the French Revolution had never happened? Or if aliens had invaded during the American Civil War?

Alternative histories have a fulcrum point where the alternative story differs from our own. Their world then develops along a different path. Sometimes there will be a science fiction blend within the story, such as time travel or inter-dimensional travel.

Time travel often goes hand in hand with the alternative fantasy and has become a popular device in fantasy romance. A good example is the 1980 film *Somewhere in Time* in which a young playwright, played by Christopher Reeve, goes back in time to find love, creating his own alternative history.

Some famous alternative history authors include Harry Turtledove, David Weber and Eric Flint, Robert Silverberg, Judith Tarr, David Drake and Naomi Novik.

Contemporary fantasy

Also known as modern-day fantasy, these stories deal with the real world, but where magic and magical creatures exist, have been discovered, or are hidden.

Three main plot devices often used are: a magical portal to other worlds, such as Marion Zimmer Bradley's *Glenraven*; a normal world but with a magical one underneath, as in J.K. Rowling's Harry Potter series; two parallel worlds meet, as in Mercedes Lackey's *Bedlam's Bard*.

Contemporary fantasy generally has a strong atmosphere and setting. It's exciting; anyone could be the hero or wizard. Your neighbour, teacher, or the snotty kid down the road. For an author there is less world-building to do, as you base your setting on the known world. The reader is comfortable, too, feeling as if they already know this world.

A word of caution: potential exists for problems within a story set in a modern world. If there are inconsistencies within your story or within the rules of magic, readers will notice and you're sure to hear about it. Be consistent in your story.

And whatever your magical elements, make certain you carry them the whole way through the story. Your magic shouldn't be so subtle that your readers question the characters and the choices they make. If the magic is too subtle, the reader won't recognise it as magic and will assume it is a normal event in your world and not something magical. You've lost a core part of your story and, in the process, diluted the reading pleasure.

On the other hand, if the magic is overwhelming, then the 'too stupid to live' tag, TSTL (seen in some so-called 'teen slasher' movies), kicks in. If the magic in your story permeates every action or reaction your character has, without any sense or rules, it forces your character to do incredibly stupid things. To use an absurd example, a wizard's stronghold is protected by the fiercest of battle mages. If the magic is too easily available, your character might attack the stronghold with, let's say, a magic spoon, the overwhelming magic resulting in ridiculous actions.

If you've watched any of the teen slasher films, and seen a girl waltz into danger, even though she's fully aware of what could happen to her, you'll know why readers tag such characters TSTL. Make sure logic and reason prevail, even in a magical setting.

You also need to ask yourself whether the contemporary setting moves the story along. If it doesn't, consider whether it's time for a magical world shift. For example, should you shift your story from a contemporary world to a totally fantastical world that you create?

Authors of contemporary fantasy include J.K. Rowling, Stephenie Meyer, Mercedes Lackey, Jim Butcher and Susan Cooper.

Urban fantasy

Urban fantasy stories usually take place within the confines of a city, although may not stay wholly within the city during the timeline of the story. Plots are either open or closed. Open plots contain magic or magical elements obvious to all. Closed stories contain magical events hidden or concealed.

Urban fantasy is a fast-growing, immensely popular genre that often ends up with its borders blurred. Other genres, like paranormal romance, may have a secondary tag of urban fantasy. In the world of an urban fantasy character, elements such as vampires, shape-shifters, demons and magic are common. Magic, danger and fast action are prominent in the story. Some will have romantic elements, but often as a side story or secondary plot.

Urban fantasies can be further divided. Traditional urban fantasy tends to involve folklore, fairy tales, and good versus evil. These stories will still be set in the modern urban world, but with a fairy-tale aspect to it. Authors include Melissa Marr, Holly Black, Charles de Lint, Mercedes Lackey and Neil Gaiman.

Then there are urban fantasies involving vampires, werewolves, elves, etc. Although some editors say such elements have been done to death, the books keep coming out and are still popular with readers, especially since the stories adapt well to both movies and television, as shows like *Buffy*, *Charmed* and *Supernatural* demonstrate.

Some urban fantasies will have kick-ass heroines with or without supernatural or magical powers. There is always a strong sense of good versus evil, detailed descriptions and, frequently, a first-person narrative. Often there will be a romantic interest for the plucky heroine, as in Nalini Singh's urban fantasy romances where angels create and rule vampires, and hunter Elena Deveraux battles seductive but lethal archangel, Raphael (*Angels' Blood*, Berkley Sensation, March 2009).

Other examples of urban fantasy authors writing about werewolves, vampires and the like are Laurell

K. Hamilton, Kim Harrison, Ilona Andrews, Kelley Armstrong, Patricia Briggs, C.E. Murphy, Rachel Vincent and Keri Arthur.

Sword and sorcery

Sword and sorcery normally involves fast-paced physical conflict. Heroes are larger than life: characters like Conan from Robert E. Howard's *Conan the Barbarian*, *Druss the Legend* by David Gemmell and even in later years, *Xena: Warrior Princess* on television. Their emotions are heightened; they enjoy life to the fullest regardless of the consequences. There can be romantic elements, but the focus is on personal battles. A magic or supernatural element is always present. Quite often, the sword-and-sorcery story develops into a series of books, although they also work well as stand-alone titles.

The term 'sword and sorcery' was coined in 1961 by American author Fritz Leiber. The term stuck and is now commonly used. Originally, sword and sorcery began in fantasy magazines and male characters dominated. Females only appeared when they needed to be rescued. Marion Zimmer Bradley changed this with her *Sword and Sorceresses* anthology. These days, female and male characters compete for equal billing within a story. Well-known sword-and-sorcery authors include Terry Brooks, Mercedes Lackey, Michael Moorcock, David Eddings, Sara Douglass.

High fantasy

High fantasy is also called epic fantasy. This is the story set in a fantasy world, either invented or parallel to our own. Serious in tone as a rule, these stories are about the epic struggle between good and evil. They often include elements such as elves, magic, wizards, quests and invented languages. The stakes and moral tones in the epic fantasy are usually high. In the high fantasy romantic 2007 film, *Stardust* from Neil Gaiman's novel, the heroine is a fallen star pursued by the hero for his own benefit. Eventually he discovers his own fate, and in the process, true love. Terry Brooks is another good example of an author writing high fantasy.

Elfpunk

Elfpunk is actually a sub-genre of urban fantasy. These are fantasy stories set in the gritty streets of a modern city environment and are peopled with faeries, elves, dragons and other beings from folklore. Authors writing elfpunk include Holly Black, Terry Brooks, and Laurell K. Hamilton with her Meredith Gentry series.

Steampunk

This sub-genre of historical fantasy is often blended with speculative fiction. Stories are set in Victorian or Edwardian times when steam power was still widely used. They contain elements of science fiction or fantasy, such as fictional technological inventions or real technological inventions invented in a much earlier time.

Although originally steampunk works were set in historical eras, we are now seeing fantasy realms with steampunk elements as opposed to historical settings that present an alternative reality. Among the best known steampunk authors are H.G. Wells and Jules Verne. Romance writers including Liz Maverick, Meljean Brooks and Gail Dayton are using steampunk in their books to revisit classic romances in a grittier way.

Heroic fantasy

Heroic fantasy generally features a hero, his life and battles. They involve complicated plots with many characters and can span different lands and worlds. Typically, heroic fantasy has always been included with sword and sorcery, but has now splintered off into its own category as its popularity has risen.

Subject matter traditionally covers big battles and conflicts, good versus evil, and the fate of worlds. Often the main character doesn't want to be the champion or hero, he just wants to be left alone. They may be serfs or farm boys who unknowingly have royal connections. They might be termed 'unexpected heroes', such as Jimmy from the book *Jimmy the Hand*, Raymond E. Feist's Legends of the Riftwar series. Jimmy was a boy thief, not known for his goodness of heart. But he helped Prince Arutha in his quest to save his poisoned wife and in the process became one of the most powerful men in the kingdom.

In heroic fantasy, events spiral out of the hero's control and he is dragged into the conflict. Responsibility is thrust upon him and he has no choice but to involve himself. He is typically tested for worthiness through both physical and mental challenges. Sometimes these stories will also involve high-fantasy crossovers and the fated quest. David Eddings, David Gemmell, Raymond E. Feist, Mercedes Lackey and Lloyd Alexander are all heroic fantasy authors.

Historical fantasy

Historical fantasies are stories set in a certain time, with magical and fantasy elements. The stories could have magic, elves, faeries and/or supernatural themes. The setting can be a factual world, time or historical point. It could also be set in a fantasy world which has recognisable (to us) historical elements in the setting or characters.

Sometimes historical events are the focus more than the time period. Light magic, or stories where the supernatural or magical elements are secondary to the history but are still present, will appear in this genre. When set within a world of the author's making, the history can be tailored to the needs of the plot, but the writer must make sure the story does not slip into alternative history.

One way to create a world is to take a belief or cultural issue and create a world around the idea. Phillip Pullman took the idea that everyone has a soul and built upon it in *The Golden Compass*. In his book, the souls of children and adults walk beside them as animals or beasts. He built his world around this one concept.

A good historical fantasy novel combines the past with magical elements or events. To produce a multi-layered story within this genre, the writer must provide history, magical elements and convincing characters, settings and plot. A variation on historical fantasy is secret history. Magic and/or magical creatures exist, but are kept secret or hidden.

Examples of historical fantasy authors are Katharine Kerr, Katherine Kurtz, David Gemmell, Naomi Novik, Stephen R. Lawhead and Diana Gabaldon.

Dark fantasy

Dark fantasy combines the elements of fantasy with horror. Some consider dark fantasy an offshoot of the horror genre, but this isn't strictly true. Dark fantasy is set around grimmer themes and can include stories of dark supernatural beings—vampires, for example —but with human motivations. These stories focus on elements of horror, but the setting is more high fantasy or sword and sorcery, whether in a fantasy or contemporary world. Bestselling romance writer Linda

Winstead Jones has crossed many genres. She ventures into dark fantasy romance in her book, *Sundown* (Silhouette Nocturne, 2009) in which bar owner, Abby, caters to humans and vampires who embrace their dark side to the point of murder, bringing detective Leo Stryker into Abby's life.

Authors writing dark fantasy include Stephen King, Clive Barker, Ann Bishop, Anne Rice, Kelley Armstrong and the queen of the 'dark' series, Christine Feehan.

Magical realism

Magical realism focuses on a story that is grounded in reality. It has a normal setting and atmosphere, but the plot may have magical or supernatural elements, either symbolic or physical.

These stories tend to be highly literary and often philosophical in nature. Although not considered magical realism, Dan Brown's novel *The Da Vinci Code* had some readers believing the book had a factual basis. Whether a good idea or not, this is the aim of magical realism: to give the reader the hope that the writer's world exists.

Magical realism employs a number of techniques:

Combinations of two or more contrasting settings: This aims to form a unique setting and/or plot, such as a rich rural setting within a gritty urban city. Another combination is a native cultural setting or plot blended with that of a European or western one.

Undue influence: The goal of magical realism is objectivity. The author's view of the world and magic should not be forced on the reader. The author has to make sure that their version of the reality portion is not compromised by their personal views, thus destroying the magical realism. For these stories to work, the magical must become ordinary and the mundane magical. The line between what is fantastic and what is real must be torn down so the magic works in tandem with reality throughout the story.

Keeping something back: Magical realism is reality with unexplained moments of magic. To explain a magical element in minute degree can make the action or object look even more unreal.

Unreal versus the real: Within magical realism the supernatural or magical elements blend subtly within the realistic world. While aware of the 'special elements', the reader should believe that things might, in the right context, actually happen that way.

Some outstanding writers of magical realism are Isabel Allende, Toni Morrison and Gabriel Garcia Marquez.

More offshoots
Other sub-genres have arisen from the fantasy genre. One deserving a mention is paranormal romance. Paranormal romances use some of the plot devices of fantasy and horror, in particular with characterisation,

whether that be shape-shifters, magic, vampires, demons or any of the other denizens of the supernatural and paranormal. More often than not these books are set in a contemporary world. The difference is that the romance between your main characters is the driving force of the story.

Many romance publishers are creating new lines to deal with increasing interest in the paranormal. Harlequin is one of these and their Luna and Nocturne imprints offer everything from fantasy and contemporary romance to urban fantasy. Other publishers, such as Baen, Tor Books, Ace Books, Kensington, Berkley Publishing Group and St Martin's Press, include paranormal romance in their lists.

Venturing into the worlds of fantasy and romance provides almost unlimited scope for storytellers to explore, provided you make sure the romance drives the story. Whatever world you choose to explore, the love story must remain key.

If you're attracted to writing within these fields, but fear being overwhelmed by the choices and challenges ahead of you, well-known Australian fantasy author Louise Cusack has this advice:

The only way to overcome fear is to focus on your goal—publication—rather than on your fear of failure. Imagine if your child ran out into the traffic. Would you be paralysed by your own fear of being hit, or would you run out without thinking? Of course you'd go after the child without a second thought, because it means so much more to you than your fear does. If writing means that much to you, don't think about the risks, just run after it.

Multi-published fantasy author KELLY ETHAN is the mother of one crazy, smart, energetic little boy who delights in driving her slightly insane. Writing is her outlet for madness and she uses it well. She started sneaking Mills & Boon books into her room at the ripe old age of fourteen and has never looked back. She reviews books for CataRomance.com and enjoys writing paranormal fantasy, fast-paced romantic stories. Kelly is currently writing an urban fantasy young adult novel and loving every minute of it! No matter the genre, she loves kick-ass, sarcastic heroines who like to save the hero and the day. The daughter of romance writer Alexis Fleming, Kelly is married to her own hero in the army and they move regularly around Australia having their own fantastical adventures. You can catch up with Kelly through her website: www.kellyethan.com.

8

KEEPING READERS
in suspense

VALERIE PARV

Long before romance novels branched out into sub-genres containing suspense, intrigue and real-life conflicts, I enjoyed writing these elements into my books. In my first romance novel, *Love's Greatest Gamble*, the heroine's late husband, a Vietnam War serviceman, was a victim of what's now called post-traumatic stress syndrome. The term may have existed then but wasn't in common use.

Unbeknown to his wife, the husband had been a compulsive gambler because of his condition. The first she knows about the problem is after his death, when the hero, owner of a large casino, arrives on her doorstep to collect on the gambling debts. To protect her daughter, who idolises her father's memory, the heroine agrees to repay the debt by marrying the hero and staying with him for a year.

The book was a gamble in more than just title. The Vietnam War was far from a popular cause, and certainly not a predictable background for a romance. But I've always been interested in why we act as we do, and this passion must have shone through, because after a few months of rewrites and polishing, the book came out in hardcover then in paperback, and has been translated any number of times.

Love's Greatest Gamble is one of my favourite novels, not only because it was my first, but also because of the psychology it let me explore. Later, in *Man Shy*, I would write about a heroine who'd been a battered wife. This book almost didn't see the light of day because of the difficulty in balancing the story elements with the developing romance.

With my London-based editor, I worked long and hard to make the book strongly romantic, while keeping the battered-wife elements true to the experiences of readers who may have been there themselves. Several times, I nearly gave up on the idea, only to be drawn back to it by the belief that true love really does conquer all. In the end, the book came out in hardcover and paperback, and became one of my most translated books over many years.

My first real venture into what we'd now call romantic suspense was *Ask Me No Questions*. After disappearing on their wedding night six years before, the hero returns on the eve of the heroine's marriage to another man. While the chemistry between them is as powerful as ever, his refusal to answer questions about where he's been strikes at the heart of their relationship, making her fear he's planning to leave her again. Although the book wasn't identified as romantic suspense, spying, international intrigue and deception provide the backdrop for the developing romance.

Nowadays, story-lines like these are far more widespread. While the relationship still forms the core of the story, romances frequently include realism, adventure, suspense, paranormal elements and eroticism.

What kind of heroines populate this fast-changing landscape? They can be rescuers in their own right, with the hero described in one set of writing guidelines as 'man enough to let himself be rescued from time to time'. Whatever their background, heroines are independent, self-assured and capable, wanting a partner to fulfil their lives rather than needing someone to take care of them.

THE ROMANTIC JOURNEY

Many years ago all the action in traditional romances stopped 'at the bedroom door'. Now, almost all romance novels, other than those aimed at the faith-based 'inspirational' lines, let the characters make love, and this is certainly true of romantic suspense. Books also reflect any stage in the romantic journey, from the so-called sweet romances where lovemaking is implied rather than shown, all the way to full-on eroticism, introducing elements of the once-forbidden or taboo.

Suspense is now one of the most popular sub-genres of romantic fiction. As well as wanting the romance to reach a successful conclusion, the reader wants the suspense thread to end satisfactorily, with justice done, villains caught and the universe saved, preferably by the direct actions of the hero and heroine.

As I discovered in my early forays into romantic suspense, the hard part is developing the romance as evenly as you develop the suspense elements. It's easy to get caught up in the adventure and forget that the romance needs to unfold in tandem.

In romantic suspense, the romance needs to be the main story thread, with the suspense carrying the two through to their happy ending. If there's too much emphasis on the suspense or adventure, with the romance unfolding as a sideline or sub-plot, the book is more properly a suspense novel with romantic elements.

Ideally the book shouldn't lean too heavily one way or the other. If the mystery becomes a minor factor in the developing romance, you lose the excitement of the suspense thread. On the other hand, if the hero and heroine quickly team up and solve the mystery together, you lose the tension of 'will they or won't they get together'.

In addition, I don't advise making either the hero or heroine the key suspect in the mystery. In the romance genre, the reader knows the hero and heroine are destined for each other, so it's tough to make either one seem as if they're the real villain. Then again, in the writing business, I'm reluctant to say never. As fast as I do, someone will write a crackerjack story that keeps us guessing whether the hero is the bad guy, or the heroine's true love, till the very end. If you're that writer, go for it, as long as you're aware of the pitfalls along the way.

NEW TERRITORY

One of my most ambitious romantic suspense projects was a three-part series called Code of the Outback. Built around the natural daughter and foster sons of a property owner in the Kimberley region of Western Australia, each book contains a complete romance as well as part of a suspense plot which wasn't resolved until the end of book three.

Although feedback was encouraging, I'm not sure I'd do this again, because of the need to read the three books in sequence to find out how the mystery plays out. And I'm still answering letters and emails about a fourth foster brother whose story was hinted at, but remained unwritten for a long time. One reader wrote, 'Please don't tell me Cade turns out to be gay'. No, he doesn't. The first three couples each had their own, unique role to play in solving the mystery, but Cade's story was never part of the suspense arc which was resolved in *Deadly Intent*. He remained 'bookless' until starring in my upcoming short story, *Never Too Late*, being published soon (*How Do I Love Thee?* Allen & Unwin, 2009).

Your plot needs to give your characters a strong, believable challenge, requiring the whole book to resolve. At the same time, the couple should have problems between themselves which stop them falling into each other's arms until almost the end of the story. I like to show the characters' romantic feelings growing at the same time as they deal with the suspense thread, as in this example from book one of Code of the Outback, *Heir to Danger*:

How long would it be before Jamal found out that [Shara] was on Diamond Downs land? Staying with Des and Judy, she had some protection. On her own in the middle of nowhere, she had none.

Not that it was any concern of his, Tom

assured himself. She might be a sloe-eyed beauty with more fire than most of the women he knew, but it didn't mean he wanted to get any more involved in her problems. Driving by the old cottage and keeping an eye on her from a discreet distance yesterday was part of his job as a ranger, nothing personal.

Now all he had to do was convince his raging hormones.

And this example from *Deadly Intent*:

She stood up, thinking that his eye on her was way too distracting for her own good. 'I'll be fine from here on.'

'What if there's another snake?'

'I have my camera stand and I'm not afraid to use it.'

'You really would stay out here alone, wouldn't you?'

In many ways she would find it easier than dealing with the disturbing way he made her feel. But the thought of him leaving wasn't comfortable either. Make up your mind what you want, she told herself.

'If we get anywhere near the mine, Horvath will turn up the heat,' Blake warned her.

A feeling of triumph flooded through her out of proportion to the victory she sensed she'd won. Blake was not only staying, he was going to help her find the lost mine. She'd have the story of her career.

She would also have to deal with the attraction simmering between herself and Blake. Anything Horvath threw at her was likely to seem tame by comparison.

'I can handle it,' she said, wishing she could be sure which challenge she was referring to.

WHAT IF?

The fusion of romance with other elements opens up exciting possibilities for writers, enabling you to write the book of your heart as editors search for new, fresh approaches to the stories.

With romances pushing the boundaries of what has been considered acceptable until now, almost any element can be included as long as the romance remains your key focus. As with all writing, you should only write what you enjoy reading, rather than trying to satisfy a market trend which may well have moved on while your book is in development.

'What if?' is a question I use regularly, both to develop a book and to solve plotting problems during the writing. An example is the reader favourite of twins switching places. Traditionally, the hero is fooled for a time at least. But what if the hero knows the twins have switched places, and decides to teach them a lesson? This question turned into the inspiration for my book *Centrefold*.

'What if a hero had arrived by UFO?' became the basis for *The Leopard Tree*. This book was originally accepted by Mills & Boon, until Alan Boon decided British readers weren't quite ready for a hero with UFO connections, and suggested I remove this element.

I felt strongly that the hero's air of mystery highlighted the sense of him being a loner, the odd man out in his society, and decided against making the change. The book was eventually published with the UFO element intact by Harlequin's sister company, Silhouette Books. Sometimes you have to wait for the market to catch up with your ideas.

Writing Code of the Outback was so satisfying that I introduced suspense elements into my fictional South Pacific kingdom of Carramer, with *Operation Monarch*. In this book, my hero was a notorious bad boy who just might be the true heir to the Carramer throne.

The heroine was the present monarch's bodyguard, assigned to the hero until the uncertainty was resolved. DNA testing was the obvious way to get at the truth. Despite what you may have seen on TV, DNA testing needs at least two weeks to complete (for now anyway), creating a suspense-filled time limit when the hero and heroine were forced to deal with the situation and each other.

The DNA testing laboratory I contacted for information was pleased to help, saying that too often writers show DNA testing happening within days. That's why I scaled the time frame of the plot to just under the required two weeks, long enough to preserve the uncertainty of the hero's background, while acknowledging forensic facts.

Later, in *Desert Justice*, I explored another reader-favourite convention, the idea of a sheikh as hero, with an Australian woman caught up in a plot against his sovereignty. Where one or the other character finds themselves falling in love in unfamiliar surroundings, the books are often described as 'fish out of water' stories. This type of plot probably appeals to me so much because it represents my own core decision at work, described in the earlier chapter on packing an emotional punch.

In *Desert Justice*, the element of suspense means the sheikh can't give in to his feelings for the heroine until the threat to both their lives is resolved, as this example shows:

He took her arm again and steered her away from the carnage. She stiffened, but told herself the touch was clinical, for her good. So why did desire leap inside her like a startled gazelle? This was getting crazy. She couldn't even fight at his side without wanting him. He might agree that women deserved equal opportunity, but he was still the sheikh, the take-charge leader. And she had never wanted him more.

ROMANTIC CONVENTIONS

When editors say they want fresh, original stories, it's tempting to think conventions such as twins, sheikhs and secret babies (one the hero doesn't know he's fathered) are old hat. But stories like these are popular for a reason. They pit the hero and heroine against each other at close quarters, on a deeply emotional level. You can use the romantic conventions provided you give them your own unique twist, and working in the suspense sub-genre provides you with ample opportunity.

The more closely you can tie in the characters' emotional needs with the suspense plot, the stronger your story will be. In *Operation Monarch*, the hero had broken the heroine's heart when they were teenagers. Now she's no longer the vulnerable young woman he once teased, but time has made the attraction stronger than ever. What is she going to do about it? How is he, a born rebel, to deal not only with her, but with possibly becoming the nation's ruler?

As we've seen, nothing in the romance world stands still, any more than real life does. My romantic suspense novels were originally published under the Silhouette Intimate Moments imprint, which is now called Romantic Suspense to more clearly signal the romantic elements readers enjoy, with what the publisher calls 'the added bonus of suspense'. Instead of the books being valued primarily as novels of suspense, reader feedback indicated they wanted more focus on the hero and heroine, and to be swept away by the unfolding love story.

As in *Operation Monarch*, the strong-willed heroines are still there, with powerful heroes to match them in every way, but the suspense elements are used to bring heightened passion and emotion into the developing relationship.

Balancing the elements demands writing skill and a thorough understanding of what makes a romance romantic: the emotional tug-of-war between the attraction the characters feel at first meeting, and the problem or conflict standing between them, seemingly never to be resolved—although we know it will be.

VIRGINS AND GUARDIANS

What doesn't work in these brave new worlds of romance? As discussed, the conventions long beloved of readers can still work provided you make them current and relevant. One character can have amnesia, or your heroine can be raising the hero's baby when they meet again.

In most communities these days, being a single parent is perfectly acceptable and no longer works as a source of conflict. It's also difficult to make a virgin heroine believable unless her reasons are spelled out so they make sense in the present day. We probably won't see many more heroes as guardians (substitute parents) of the heroine, who is totally subject to his control. In place of this device, we might find a hero and heroine sharing a property or business for whatever reason; deciding to share parenthood once the hero learns he is a father; or one turning to the other for a makeover, sexual adventure, or to resolve some other mutual need.

In line with the trend to increased eroticism, characters don't need to be shown worrying about their sexual impulses. Provided the sex is consensual, there's no need for apologies afterwards, and safe sex should be openly practised. In other words, as with the rest of society, characters are more sure of themselves and less dependent on others to justify or explain their behaviour.

The heroine whose biological clock is ticking madly can look for a man to father her child without expecting marriage, although this may well be the outcome once they get to know each other.

Along with contemporary values, writers should also take technology into account. Our characters need to live in the real world. This means dealing with everything from mobile phones, the internet, VOIP, CSI, laptops, Blackberries and blogs, to whatever else is invented in the millisecond since writing this. As I found with *Operation Monarch*, I couldn't ignore the reality of DNA testing simply to create uncertainty about the father of the heroine's child.

Although Code of the Outback was set in one of the most remote parts of Western Australia, people in the region still have access to satellite communications and the internet. Few people are so isolated that they don't have these facilities, unless by choice, so if you want to make your characters dependent on their own resources, you need to factor in flat mobile phone batteries, or some other plausible explanation.

CHECK THE BALANCE

As stated, balancing the elements of romance and suspense can be tricky. It's a good idea to check the publisher's tip sheets (writer's guidelines) or scroll through the FAQs on their websites to see what is considered ideal. Some publishers say they prefer a fifty–fifty mix of romance and suspense, others sixty–forty, with the emphasis on the emotional growth of the characters.

The best way to see how this works in practice is to read current books in the line you wish to target. Highlighting the scenes in two colours—one for romance, the other for suspense—lets you see the mix at a glance.

Both plot lines need to intertwine so one can't exist without the other. For example, if the hero and heroine are former army buddies who served in the same unit together, this could make them the target of a common enemy. Realising their other comrades are being picked off one by one, they may have to team up to stay alive, forcing them into an intimacy neither welcomes.

The villain you have opposing them should also be strong and believable. We should understand why they do what they do, even if we don't agree with their methods. Depending on the length of the book, the villain needs to have a life apart from their interaction with the hero and heroine.

While the hero and heroine are trying to track down the villain or second-guess their next move, what is the villain doing? Are they aware of being tracked? Setting a trap to lure the good guys in? Too often the bad guys are put in a box and only taken out when they're needed.

A good way to study the villain's role is to think of a villain you love to hate, perhaps from a movie or TV series. List the characteristics that make this person such a good villain. What do you think motivates them to behave as they do?

EMOTIONAL CONNECTION

When creating your romantic suspense plot, try to develop a story that provides an emotional connection between the hero and heroine right from the beginning. In *Operation Monarch*, the heroine was a society girl who knew the hero when they were in high school together and he was the bad boy from the wrong side of the tracks. She'd harboured a secret fancy for him all along, and one day he'd kissed her, setting all her teenage hormones raging, until she found out he'd kissed her on a dare.

She learned that he despised everything she stood for, her apparently easy life of trading on her looks as a model, his not knowing her parents had pushed her into modelling. The hero's antipathy gave her the courage to stand up for herself and make her own life as an adult.

When they meet again in the story's present, she's skilled in martial arts and working as a bodyguard for the country's monarch. When suspicion arises that the hero is the country's true ruler, once believed to have died at birth, they're forced to deal with each other until the truth can be established. The old issues between them can't be ignored, and must be resolved if they're to have a chance at future happiness.

This story establishes an emotional connection between the hero and heroine from page one. Their shared history and his effect on her, which she is stunned to learn hasn't lessened with time, set the passions sizzling as soon as they set eyes on each other after years apart.

While their shared past makes it easier to show the attraction building between them, you have to be careful about taking time out from a crisis to let them get flirtatious. It's better to create spaces in the tension when they can safely and logically face their growing feelings. In *Operation Monarch*, they were sent to a summer palace while they awaited the results of the genetic testing:

'I recommend setting up a command post at the summer palace at Allora, where it would be easier to keep the investigation under wraps,' Serena proposed.

Lorne inclined his head. 'I concur. The two of you will go there as soon as the [DNA] testing is complete.'

The two of you.

Instant heat coiled through her, disturbing in its intensity. Basing the investigation at Allora was logical and Garth had to be involved, but she hadn't counted on Lorne sending Garth to the summer palace with her. Already her aware-ness of him put her senses on overdrive. Tough to function efficiently when unsettling currents ripped through her every time he looked at her.

If your characters are holed up somewhere waiting for the villain to show, make sure the setting provides scope for emotional development as well as heightening suspense. For example, give them a motel with only one room available, with a double bed and a mirrored ceiling. Not the sort of place they'd normally prefer, but they have no choice. How do they handle the setting in terms of the romance? Do they feel the attraction is appropriate? Wish for a better time and place? Make the most of the opportunity?

In writing the scene, you would need to show all these conflicts through their viewpoints so we are aware of their growing emotional tension. Keeping them together as much as possible forces them to deal with their emotions as well as with the conflict between them.

Stepping up the conflict as a counterpoint to the increasing emotional tension will help to avoid the dreaded 'sagging middle' in your plot. Taking the earlier example, if the hero and heroine were in the military together, and were tempted to make love, why didn't they? Rank? Fear of getting entangled because someone the heroine once loved had been killed soon after they made love, making her edgy about loving and losing?

What if the hero then gets captured or injured, forcing her to accept that living is risky, she can't control what happens, she can only live in the now, and decides that's the best course. If you like, try writing this scene between two characters of your own invention and see what happens. Make sure you focus on the attraction between them, contrasting with the conflict keeping them apart.

GOAL, MOTIVATION, CONFLICT

In her book *Goal, Motivation, Conflict: The Building Blocks of Good Fiction* (Gryphon Books for Writers, 1996), Debra Dixon sums up the essential elements every character—including your villains—should have in order to come to life in your story. (I think this book deserves to be on every writer's bookshelf, and have seen copies selling at online auctions for as much as $300. The book can be bought far more reasonably at the publisher's website, www. gryphonbooksforwriters.com.)

Using the GMC approach, whether your characters are kick-butt secret agents, or have magical abilities or vampire tendencies, we still need to know *what* they want (their goal), *why* they want it (motivation) and *what's stopping them* from attaining their goal (conflict).

In addition, each key character should have an internal and an external version of their GMC. For example, in *Operation Monarch*, the heroine's goals are to rise through the ranks of the royal protection service (external) and convince the hero there's more to her than the air-headed clothes horse he knew as a teenager (internal). The hero's goals are to prove he was wrongly dishonourably discharged from the navy (external), establish that he's no prince (external), and show the heroine how he has always felt about her (internal). The villain wants revenge on the royal family for once treating him badly (external), and seeks power through destabilising the throne (internal).

Some of the characters' motivations can already be seen in the examples given. The heroine is motivated by ambition and desire; the hero wants justice from the navy, and perhaps from society for the bad hand he has been dealt; the villain wants revenge and status/power.

As an exercise, you might like to choose the key characters from a book, movie or film, or from your own work, and try to work out their internal and external goals, motivations and conflicts. Then see how closely you can link their stories together, as I did by making the heroine the hero's bodyguard in *Operation Monarch*.

In your story, could the heroine turn out to be the hero's ex-wife, for instance? Or the woman he scorned when he was on his way up as an ambitious young turk? Is she now a rich woman in her own right? Did they have a one-night stand years ago, resulting in a child he doesn't know about? If she has a baby, how can she be a virgin, a fact she can no longer conceal when they make love? This was the basis of the conflict in my romance *Booties and the Beast*.

The more closely you can interweave the conflicts, the stronger will be your story. In *Operation Monarch*, the hero and heroine were attracted years before, now their relative positions put them at odds while throwing them close together. The villain has a history no one knows about until he shows his hand.

The higher the stakes and the more intense the emotions the characters experience, the easier it is to balance the romance with suspense. The hero and heroine must not only win the day, they must learn to love and trust into the bargain, not an easy task. But if you can combine the two in a compelling love story, you'll not only keep your readers in suspense, they'll love every minute of it.

Find out more about Valerie Parv's writing by visiting www. valerieparv.com.

9

THE BIG 'O':
Opportunities in erotic romance

ALEXIS FLEMING

When I started writing, I had no doubt that I would write romance. Whether set in this world or a fantasy world I created, romance was it. I read across all the sub-genres within the romance spectrum, but fantasy romance was my first love. I never actually set out to write erotic romance. Little did I know!

I'd always written hot when it came to my love scenes. I never was able to close that bedroom door. Hey, what can I say? I like sex and I've always felt it was part of the whole romance package. I adore writing the love scenes, so why deprive my reader? Why not allow them to share in the fantasy as well?

Even before I started writing erotic romance, my stories were highly sensual. One of my editors said it was like reading pages of foreplay that upped the sexual tension before the characters even got to the main event.

When my critique partner suggested I write an erotic romance, I told her that I couldn't even say the word 'pussy' without laughing, let alone write it. She told me to go away and practise. About a week later, as a joke, I sent her an instant message by computer. I'd filled the whole screen with one word, over and over again. One guess what that word was? Unbeknown to me, her grown-up son was working on her computer when the message came in. He read it, started laughing, and called his mother. 'Hey, Mum, I think this one's for you.'

I was mortified when I found out. Embarrassing, yes, but it did get me thinking about writing erotic romance and, before I knew it, I was writing erotic romantic comedies and getting them published.

WHAT IS EROTIC ROMANCE?

For a while now, I've been trawling the internet, reading books, talking to people, and trying to settle on a concise definition of erotic romance, but the definition varies according to whom you're speaking.

Ellora's Cave, a well-known publisher of erotic romance, has coined a word that I think defines it, at least for me: *romantica*, which is a combination of romance and erotica. A red-hot, sizzling, make-you-squirm-on-your-seat romance. And the most important word in that sentence: romance.

Erotic or not, first and foremost the story must be a good romance. Add in all the explicit sex and graphic language you want, but if you don't have a well-developed romance at the centre of the plot, guess what, folks? You're not writing an erotic romance.

Let's concentrate on romance for a bit. First off, what *is* a romance? At its most basic, it's a story centred around a love relationship and the conflicts within that relationship. Romance novels are about emotions and a journey towards love and commitment.

In erotic romance, this love relationship does not necessarily have to mean a hero and heroine. Erotic romance has evolved to include many lifestyles, from heterosexual to homosexual, bisexual, or any combination thereof. Regardless of gender, what we need to craft is a great romance.

One word of caution: if you find it difficult to read erotic romance books, maybe writing them isn't for you. If you're not comfortable with it, believe me, your editor will know, and so will your readers.

A FINE ROMANCE

What do we need to write a good romance novel? I start with some of the basics.

A strong plot: A plot containing the four Cs: Conflict, Complication, Crisis, Conclusion. A story arc strong enough to sustain the whole story for however many words are necessary to bring the story to its conclusion.

An engaging hero and heroine: A hero we can fall in love with. A heroine we can empathise with. Three-dimensional characters who drag us into the story and keep us there until the end.

Now, don't beat me over the head when I use *hero* and *heroine*. For the sake of simplicity, I'm talking generalities here.

A satisfying ending: The happily-ever-after (sometimes shortened to HEA) or, if you prefer, the happy-for-now scenario. A romance novel doesn't have to end in marriage, but we want to be able to imagine that these two people have some type of shared future.

Forward movement: Every scene in a romance must do one of three things: develop the characters, develop the internal or external conflicts, or develop the romance. The focus in a romance novel is always the romance.

Structural strength: In this regard, erotic romance is no different. It needs to have a beginning, a middle and an end, the same strong plot and engaging characters. Erotica is usually centred on sex. Romance is about love and emotional relationships, of which sex is often a part. When I write erotic romance, I'm combining these elements.

DEFINING CATEGORIES

Two erotic romance authors in particular have influenced my own writing—Angela Knight and Kate Douglas. If you haven't read their work, rush out and buy one of their books. You won't be disappointed.

Angela Knight has come up with a set of definitions which are the best I've heard and kindly gave me permission to quote from her book *Passionate Ink: A Guide to Writing Erotic Romance* (Loose Id, 2007):

Pornography: created with the sole purpose of creating sexual arousal in the reader as an aid to masturbation. The main character is usually a male with multiple partners. The story does not end in a monogamous relationship. Complicated plots, well-drawn characterisation, and beautiful writing are rare, since readers are involved with the story for only a few minutes at a time.

Erotica: sexually explicit fiction with a more literary bent. A male hero is typical. Plot and characterisation are better developed than in porn, and the writing style is literate. However, stable relationships are usually not formed between characters; there are rarely the 'Happy endings' you'd find in the romance genre.

Women's erotica: more akin to literary erotica than to romance. The main character is a woman who is a strong, well-developed character. She's on a voyage of self-discovery that may include experimentation with sexual practices such as bondage and submission, and she will often have more than one partner. These books may not end with the formation of a monogamous couple, though some of them do.

Mainstream romance: the focus is on the formation of a monogamous romantic relationship between a heterosexual couple. Characterisation is key, as is plot and romantic conflict. Sex may or may not be portrayed on the page, but if it is, it's given less focus than other plot elements. The language is euphemistic, with a careful avoidance of four-letter words. There are rarely more than three love scenes in a novel, and they're often short, usually only a few pages at most. The hero and heroine form a monogamous married couple by the end of the story. This kind of ending, called a Happily Ever After (HEA), is not only expected but demanded by editors and romance readers.

Erotic Romance: as in conventional romance, the focus of the story is on the foundation of a romantic relationship between well-developed characters, but the love scenes receive more attention. There are more of them, and they are more detailed. Sex also plays an important role in driving the plot, which must be structured to allow for earlier and more frequent love scenes. The language tends to be blunter, with fewer euphemisms. As in traditional [romances], an HEA [Happily Ever After] is critical.

There's one more definition I'd like to include:

Sexy romance: stories that focus on the development of a romantic relationship that just happens to have more explicit sex. Because the sex is not an inherent part of the character growth or the relationship development, in most cases it can be removed, or toned down, without damaging the story. Happily-ever-after is a must as this is basically a standard romance with hotter sex. The language is usually not as graphic as in an erotic romance, although I notice in some of the current Harlequin Blaze books slightly more graphic terms are being used, but sparingly.

WRITING EROTIC ROMANCE

Romance is what separates straight erotica from erotic romance. Now we've established that we're writing a romance, what do we need to focus on?

First and foremost: plot. Like any good romance, you must have a strong plot. A series of sexual encounters isn't going to get you through. Yes, you might titillate the reader, but there's no story. Once the climax is over, pun intended, what's to stop the reader putting the book down and walking away? We want to hold them to the very last word. So we need a story arc.

We need a hero and a heroine. I do mean a hero. Nothing he does should portray him as less than heroic. And as for the heroine? We don't want to see a ball-buster, for want of a better title. She can start out that way, but we'd better see her changing as the story goes on or you'll lose your reader.

Also remember that erotic romance covers a much broader spectrum than the conventional one man and one woman. There is a high demand from the reader for alternative lifestyle romance. Male/male stories are very popular, as are ménages (whether it be male/male/female or female/female/male), lesbian relationships, and every combination in between.

Dumping sex scenes into a standard romance won't turn your story into an erotic romance. The sex must be part of the story arc. This is why many authors of erotic romance often find it easier to start with a sexy premise in the first place. The sex is woven into the plot from the outset.

In my first print novel, *Stud Finders Incorporated*, I employed a simple but sexy premise. I was visiting a friend in New Zealand and spotted a black box sitting on her kitchen counter. It was still in its original wrapper and right across the front was the name of the machine: stud finder. That gave me the idea for my story. Here's the cover blurb for that one:

Wanted: An Orgasm . . . and the chance to fulfil all her sexual fantasies.

Madison believes she's frigid. Her ex told her so and maybe it's true, because there's one thing she's never experienced. An orgasm! Now she wants it all. So when her mother rings Stud Finders Incorporated and hires a stud for her to practice on, why look a gift horse in the mouth?

Jake's ex-lover said he was boring, both in bed and out. So when sexy Madison asks him to teach her to have an orgasm, he jumps at the chance to prove his manhood. Even if it means hiding the fact that the purpose of Stud Finders Incorporated is to find the studs behind the wallboards of a building so the owner can safely hang his paintings.

The sex was an integral part of the story right from the word go and the book was classed as erotic contemporary romance. Create three-dimensional characters, a strong plot and a satisfying romance. Focus on those points first and let the sex come naturally as the characters dictate. Simply having them jump into bed and fitting tab A into slot B isn't enough. Tossing in all the words our mothers used to wash our mouths out for when we were kids won't turn your story into an erotic romance. As with any romance, your characters need to have a strong motivation for making love.

The reader wants to share the emotions and the build-up of tension until the point when your characters make love. Yes, your sex scenes have to be graphic and they certainly happen with greater frequency and usually a whole lot sooner in an erotic romance than in a conventional romance, but you mustn't short-change your reader. Don't make the story a clinical discussion of what fits where. If you're not turning yourself on as you write, you're not going to push your reader's buttons either.

NAUGHTY WORDS

Another important aspect to consider is the graphic language used in erotic romances. Those 'naughty' words we were never supposed to utter. Don't overdo it. Used in the right place, graphic words can punch the tension up, but if every time your hero opens his mouth, he uses the f-bomb, it's going to start annoying your reader. The language should be interwoven into the love scenes to increase the erotic component of the story.

An erotic romance isn't just a bonk a page. Each sex scene should move the story along, furthering the plot, the romance or, better yet, both! If you can lift the sex scene out of the story without damaging the flow of the story, that sex scene isn't needed. It should be integrated into the story-line.

Don't tell your readers what the heroine is feeling. Show them. Let them feel it, too. Take them along for the ride. Use the emotions, the five senses. Your love scenes shouldn't be play-by-play diagrams or a clinical discussion of the sex act. We all know how it works.

I've learned that a lot—make that most—readers are turned off by the use of clinical and anatomical terms for body parts and the sex act. They want to get down and dirty. They want to hear it like it is. Use the street terms, the graphic language we've all heard. This is part of what the reader expects. If they're buying an erotic romance, they want a romance, but they expect to find that romance hot, graphic and down to earth.

I never really was a potty mouth. I got better as I got older. Yes, I can trot out all the relevant words, but it wasn't easy for me when I started writing specifically for the erotic romance market. I grew up with an alcoholic father who used swear words to put down my mother. It took me a long time before I saw some of those words as sexy.

There are some words I still find it difficult to use, or if I include them, I only use them in the male point of view. The c-word is one I still can't say. I've used it once or twice in my stories, but only from the male POV, and I have to admit I only used it at my editor's prompting.

There's nothing wrong with using any word if you're comfortable with it, and sometimes the language can be a total turn-on for the reader. Here's a scenario. You have a prim and proper heroine who is totally turned on by what the hero is making her feel. Suddenly, in the heat of the moment, she moans and uses graphic language to urge him on. Oh yeah, our hero is going to give her all he's got! And if you realised how hard it was to write that scenario without actually using the terms, you'd be laughing right about now.

If you find it difficult using street language, then practise like I did with my critique partner. Check the publishers out. Their websites and submission guidelines usually specify the degrees of sensuality they want from writers, from the sexy, sensual romance, right up to the erotic romance.

One thing to remember: don't be tempted to use purple prose, those words and phrases that sound stilted, overly descriptive, or clichéd. Yes, we've all read it and we've all had a chuckle. Forget the clichés and go for nitty-gritty realism.

One way of identifying purple prose is by your reaction when you read it. Does it make you laugh? Or does it make you shake your head in disgust? If it does either, it's not what the editor, or the reader, is looking for.

TOO MUCH SEX?

Page after page of nothing but sex can get boring after a while. This is where plot comes in. A strong plot will carry the sex and keep the reader interested. Then the sex becomes part of the plot, rather than the most important part of the story.

The sex has to move the plot forward, otherwise it's just gratuitous. There has to be motivation for the characters to have sex.

In most of my stories, I tend to include a little bit of intrigue, an element of danger, without even being aware I'm doing it. That's the way the story plots out for me. It took me a while to realise that elements like danger and intrigue not only punch up the tension, but stop the sex taking over while keeping my romance on line.

Whichever way you craft your story, make certain it has that strong plot because sex alone won't carry the story. And for heaven's sake, don't have your characters stop to have sex when the killer is about to jump them. That's one quick way to halt the forward momentum of the story.

SEXUAL TENSION

Don't forget sexual tension. I don't mean the actual mechanical act of having sex. I mean the build-up of the tension between the characters, whatever their sex, before they actually get to the main event. Every brush of his hand, his very nearness, his body heat, his smell . . . it all combines to increase your heroine's awareness of the hero.

The same applies to the hero. Men may not articulate emotions as well or as readily as women do, but they feel them nevertheless. Give your protagonists an awareness of each other throughout the whole story. Then up the tension even more. Throw a spanner in the works. Is there an element of uncertainty, danger, conflict, whether external or internal? It all ups the tension and the awareness between the characters and makes the sex so much more poignant when it does happen.

I think, for women anyway, sex starts in the mind. You've heard of brain sex? That's what I'm talking about. As a rule, men don't need to feel the emotions to perform. It's a biological function. Show them a set of naked breasts and things start to rise.

For women, it's different. We have to feel the emotions, process what we're feeling, and then the body takes over, hormones go on the rampage and our libido spikes. The mind plays a huge role in what turns us on. How about that long-held fantasy you've harboured? Do you fantasise about a threesome or sex with a stranger? It doesn't matter what the fantasy is as long as it pushes your buttons. If it turns you on, it will do the same for your readers.

It's the writer's job to elicit an emotional response in the reader. In erotic romance, we want the response to be sensual as well as emotional. The best way to do that is to create those emotions in your characters and drag the reader along with you.

Don't just have your characters jumping into bed because you think you need a love scene. What's the purpose of a particular love scene? Is there clear motivation for them to make love at that point? Will the love scene advance the plot, or bring about some type of emotional change in your characters? If you can lift the love scene out of the story and not destroy the flow, it's not needed at that point.

Do make certain what you have your characters doing is physically possible. I once had a heroine about to make love and realised she still had her panties on. Bit hard to fit tab A into slot B while she's still partially dressed. In another manuscript I realised that my hero must have had three arms to do what he was doing at the time.

UPPING THE HEAT

Erotic romance is about pushing the boundaries, upping the heat level and maybe exploring your own fantasies. It's time to let your libido run amok.

If you like to mix genres, erotic romance is the perfect vehicle. Many authors will mix the romance with fantasy, science fiction or paranormal elements, for instance. Try a little BDSM, or a ménage. Check out some of the sex-toy sites on the internet. Hey, you're pushing the limits here.

There *are* boundaries you can't cross. Remember, we're writing a romance. Most publishing sites for erotic romance will include the baddies on the submission page of their website, but generally they'll specify:

- no paedophilia
- no rape as titillation
- no bodily functions
- no necrophilia
- no bestiality.

Erotic romance doesn't always have to mean kinky. Some authors find it easier than others to get into the more adventurous forms of sex. A lot of us grow into it the longer we write erotic romance. Don't be afraid to try something new. Hit the internet. You can find out almost anything you want there about sex. Probably more than you want to know.

There are many good how-to books on the market, and I don't just mean books on writing erotic romance. Get yourself a book or two on the psychology of sex, or books that show you a 101 different sex positions you can use in your writing. My husband still laughs every time he sees a copy of the *Kama Sutra* sitting on my desk, but that's okay because this is all about educating ourselves in order to make our erotic romance come alive on the page.

Read other authors to study their writing techniques. The more you read, the more comfortable you'll feel. Pick up books by well-known authors such as Angela Knight, Kate Douglas, Sylvia Day, Shelley Laurenston, Emma Holly, Jordan Summers and—okay—Alexis Fleming. There are many good authors to choose from.

Something I learned from Kate Douglas is that a story can be highly erotic without having to have a so-called 'dirty' word every second sentence. Kate's books illustrate everything I've mentioned. They are romantic, highly sensual, erotic with very graphic sex and emotional journeys for the reader as well as the characters.

Whether you choose to use 'vanilla' sex or have your characters get off on a little kink, make the sex count. Make it sizzle. Invite your reader to squirm along with the heroine as the hero turns her on and gets down and dirty with her. For me, this is what erotic romance is all about. Regardless of the sub-genre you write in, first and foremost, it's all about the romance!

WHERE TO NEXT?

The digital market is well suited to erotic romance and there are many publishers catering to the needs of readers who may be too embarrassed to go into a bricks-and-mortar bookstore to buy an erotic story. Heck, there are people out there who give us a hard time for buying a romance, let alone an erotic romance.

The younger generation in particular has embraced the digital market and as the cost of digital reading devices comes down, I think more people will jump on the e-book bandwagon. I buy my books online because it's convenient for me. Running a motel, I don't get out a lot, particularly during the busy season, so online shopping is easier. Incidentally, I buy all my print books online for the same reason and just have them shipped to me.

WHY E-BOOKS?

I never planned to submit to an electronic publisher. I was still submitting exclusively to print publishers when I got involved in the hospitality industry four years ago. The problem is, I tend to be a bit hot-headed at times. After an argument with my husband as to priorities and whether or not my writing was going to sell (at this point I'd only had short stories published in Australian national magazines), in a fit of pique I fired off a submission to one of the e-publishers I'd been researching. Within two hours, I had a response.

They sent me a contract on the strength of my synopsis and first three chapters. Small-minded, I know, but I couldn't help waking hubby up and dishing out a little I-told-you-so.

My career snowballed, and a little over three years later, I'm published with four different companies, in both e-book and print formats. What a buzz for the ego, but digital publishing provides additional benefits that I discovered after having my first book accepted in August 2005.

Instant gratification is one. You'll hear back from a digital publisher/editor a lot sooner than you will from most major print publishers. Monthly pay cheques are another. There's nothing like being paid monthly instead of waiting for that six-monthly royalty statement. You'll also build your confidence for later on if you sell to a 'big' print house.

Getting published can be daunting. Writing the book may well be the easiest part. Once you've been accepted, you find yourself writing blurbs and tag lines, thinking about what you'd like to see on your cover (and e-publishers usually give you a lot of flexibility when it comes to the cover art), deciding whether to use a pen name, going through editing with your editor, learning about online promotion. It's mind-boggling, but it's a lot of fun and immensely exciting.

It's easier to learn the ropes of the publishing business in a small pond. That 'smaller classroom' carries a lot of benefits and prepares you for when you hit the big time.

A note here: whether or not to use a pen name is something every writer of erotic romance will have to decide. I chose to use a pen name mainly because I wanted to keep my business endeavours separate from my writing life. I'm not ashamed or embarrassed by what I write, but I decided it was better to separate my writing persona from my everyday life.

WHERE TO DO IT

All it requires to find erotic romance publishers is a Google search. A word of warning though. Please thoroughly check out the publisher before you submit. Go to their website, get a list of their authors and contact them. Ask around your writing groups. Check with your friends and find out what their dealings have been like with the publisher. As an added precaution, check Predators & Editors (anotherealm.com/prededitors/).

WHEN TO DO IT

Keep an eye on timing for seasonal submissions. Most digital publishers will call for submissions for Christmas, Halloween, etc. and have a definite cut-off and response date. Also, watch the publisher's website for calls for submissions for contests. Those, too, have a quick turnaround and help you jump the slush pile (the name usually given to the piles of unsolicited manuscripts cluttering every publisher's office).

FROM DIGITAL TO PRINT

Now is probably the best time to try to break into erotic romance writing. Many of the digital publishers, for example Samhain Publishing, release their books in print some months after the story has come out in digital format. Once again, a check of the publisher's website will provide this information.

The 'big' publishing houses in New York have realised erotic romance is a lucrative market and now include erotic romances in their line-up. Quite a number of e-book authors have made the jump from e-book to print after being approached by the print houses to submit to them. Angela Knight is one such author who comes to mind.

Some of the publishers to look at include:

Red Sage Publishing publishes erotic romance anthologies called *Secrets*. They also now have an e-book imprint for erotic romance.

Kensington Publishing Corporation has their *Aphrodisia* line to showcase their erotic romance.

Avon Books has its own line of erotic romance imprints called *Avon Red*.

Berkley Publishing calls theirs *Berkley Heat*.

Harlequin has come out with the erotic *Spice* novels. They also have a digital imprint called *Spice Briefs*. Then there's their popular *Blaze* series for those who like things a little tamer but still highly sensual.

This is by no means a comprehensive list, but a check of the publishing sites will soon tell you which houses publish erotic romance.

Whether you prefer heterosexual, homosexual, bisexual or any combination of these, if erotic romance is your thing, the markets are out there. The opportunities are there for those who persevere. Like me, you may discover a whole other side to yourself as a writer.

Multi-published author ALEXIS FLEMING admits to being a little strange and a lot quirky. Her world is peopled with interesting characters and exciting possibilities that come to life in every book she writes. Her first love has always been romance—hot, sizzling relationships with a dash of comedy, and a few trials and tribulations thrown in to test her characters. She writes sassy, fun, erotic contemporary novels as well as paranormals and fantasies where readers come face to face with anything from sexy shifters to beings from other planets. She is published in digital format and print, by both American and British publishers. When she isn't creating sizzling tales to tempt her readers, Alexis brainstorms ideas with her daughter, fantasy romance writer Kelly Ethan.

Alexis also helps her personal hero run a large motel situated on the edge of a national marine park in Australia. She loves to hear from her readers at www.alexisfleming.net.

10

SECRET PLEASURES:
The heart of the genre

DAPHNE CLAIR

Writing romance is a feminist act.

If you write romance, expect your feminist friends to be horrified at your betrayal of the sisterhood, literary ones to ask you when you plan to write a *real* book, and casual acquaintances to say, 'So, you just change the characters' names for each book?'

Most people don't intend to be rude, although it's difficult to think otherwise of the woman who listened to a talk I gave her writing group and, afterwards, interrupted my conversation with several other people to state, 'I've never read a Mills & Boon. They're all rubbish anyway!' before stalking away.

How she knew this, never having read one, I don't

know, but her unsupported pronouncement on the books is all too common.

Romance is almost exclusively a female genre, and for centuries women's literature was assumed to be inferior to that produced by men. Even now romance novels—almost exclusively written, read and even edited by women—are still unthinkingly dismissed by the majority of academics and most media as unworthy of serious attention.

The vast majority of romance readers are voracious and eclectic readers. Like myself and other constant readers, they probably compulsively read the labels on sauce bottles and cereal packets.

WHO READS ROMANCE?

Romance readers, according to surveys conducted in the UK and US, cover the entire spectrum of woman-hood, and match almost exactly the median of those who don't read romance. There are as many doctors, lawyers, bus drivers, librarians, university lecturers, freezing workers, businesswomen, nurses and shop assistants among romance readers as in the general population of women. A couple of American studies suggest they are less likely to watch TV than the 'norm', though they're slightly more likely to be interested in politics—and in sex (a chicken-and-egg conclusion?).

To some feminist theorists, the entire romance genre is masochistic, reactionary trash that lulls readers into accepting lives of drudgery, submissiveness and deadly dullness, reinforcing an outmoded and oppressive patriarchal system. Its heroines are passive ninnies waiting for a man to come along and offer them marriage, only to turn them into barefoot, perpetually pregnant house-slaves. And romance heroes, say these theorists, are male chauvinist boors and brutes. Oddly, these same books are also supposed to give women unrealistically high expectations of their real-life partners. Which perhaps says something about many real-life men.

Either way, it seems, romance will stunt readers' personalities, rot their brains, and turn them into mindless morons—a kind of non-surgical lobotomy. Women being obviously unable to distinguish between their reality and their reading.

Anyone who believes that hasn't been reading the same books I have.

A disconcerting number of female writers—from the distinguished nineteenth-century novelist 'George Eliot', who used an alias to disguise her sex, to Germaine Greer and onward—have been quite vitriolic in their condemnation of the entire genre. Yet it continues to sell millions of copies every day.

Our books cross racial, cultural and geographical barriers, as well as cater for age groups from nine to ninety-nine. In North America nearly 9000 romance titles were released in 2007. Of book readers polled in 2007, one in five read romance novels. Harlequin alone sold over 130 million books worldwide in that year and publishes more than 120 titles a month in twenty-nine languages and 107 international markets. (Occasionally I receive a translated copy of one of my books in a language I can't figure out, published in a city I've never heard of.)

In the light of the numbers, I'm surprised at how many women, whenever Harlequin or Mills & Boon come up in conversation, feel compelled to declare loudly that they have never read one, or they 'don't read that stuff' (sometimes adding hastily when they realise I write 'that stuff' that their sister, neighbour or even grandmother does).

All those sisters, neighbours and grandmothers are presumably responsible for the genre's phenomenal sales. And those figures don't even take account of a thriving used-book market, nor books loaned or given away. It's been calculated that each paperback romance is read an average of eight times before being discarded.

I have met readers in certain occupations who live in fear of their secret pleasure being discovered by their colleagues, afraid disclosure may harm their professional reputation and chances of advancement. Even some romance writers with other 'day jobs' don't dare 'come out'. And one requested that her publisher not send her author copies because her family were so dismissive of her chosen occupation. No wonder successful author and chronicler of the romance genre Jayne Ann Krentz wrote in *Dangerous Men and Adventurous Women* (University of Pennsylvania Press, 1992): 'The fact that so many women persist in reading and enjoying romance novels in the face of generations of relentless hostility says something profound . . . about women's courage . . .'

WHY IS ROMANCE SO WIDELY DERIDED?

If men read romance at all, most simply don't understand what's going on in them—just as they famously don't understand women. So they are generally dismissive of romance novels or even actively hostile. Some academics instil that scorn in many female students, some of whom go on to write strangely fanciful (dare I say almost hysterical?) diatribes against other women's liking for it. Myths and theories abound, from the proposition that the heroes of romances are mother figures (*really?*), to the assumption that the readers are frustrated spinsters/housewives or near-illiterates, to a bizarre judgement that romance novels 'fail' because they do not provide for the reader 'a comprehensive program for reorganising her life' (Janice Radway, *Reading the*

Romance: Women, Patriarchy and Popular Literature, Chapel Hill: University of North Carolina Press, 1984) or 'a full and challenging model for human life' (Kay Mussell, *Fantasy and Reconciliation*, Greenwood Press, 1984). (Is that the function of fiction? Well, duh!)

The male bank clerk, truck driver, factory worker or professor can immerse himself in tales of espionage, terrorism, warfare, murder and mayhem without incurring the opprobrium levelled at readers of books about lasting love and commitment. No bookseller will make disparaging remarks about his purchase while wrapping it (and taking his money), and all but the most specialised bookstores will stock his favourite relaxation reading, rather than turn him away with a patronising, '*We* don't sell *that* kind of thing.'

No one will cross the street to tell him what rubbish he is reading (as happened to a friend of mine studying the romance genre for her postgraduate degree). Nor will anyone assume that his chosen relaxation reading is irrefutable proof that he has the intelligence of a gnat and expects his life to resemble a techno-thriller, science fiction adventure or new-noir detective story.

Women reading romance supposedly identify with the heroine in the books, so should I presume that men who read male-oriented books identify with protagonists who are beaten up, tortured in imaginative ways, and stabbed or shot before they defeat the enemy and save the world—or at least their own skins? Vicariously a man may fancy being a James Bond or Rambo, but unless he's in the police or armed forces he won't go out looking for gun-toting, knife-wielding villains or sinister terrorists to bring to justice.

For many women it's enjoyable to read about a tall, handsome, confident, capable, strong-but-sensitive and maybe wealthy yet highly principled man. A man other men respect, who treats women to old-fashioned courtesies and can always find a handy parking space or taxi, yet will also wash dishes, rustle up a decent meal or soothe a crying baby, and who always looks sexy, whether in a tux or a towel—or nothing at all.

That doesn't mean these women believe such a being actually exists on the planet. Women in general are nothing if not realistic. But when a woman's reality is dirty nappies and endless cooking and cleaning, or juggling a career and children, or trying to smash through the glass ceiling in a corporate or academic environment, who but she is more in need of a man who will take her away from all that—if only for a couple of hours between the pages of a book?

With all their attributes, even romantic heroes are not perfect. They can be hot-tempered, have rigid views, judge others too harshly, be embittered or prejudiced or even vengeful. What they are not is weak, even if physically handicapped—as many heroes have been throughout the genre's history. And at heart they are decent, secretly vulnerable human beings. The same goes for the heroines. It's an equal match, and even larger-than-life heroes with excess machismo will eventually be brought low by love—and by strong heroines.

THE POSSIBILITY OF LOVE

Readers are well aware that love doesn't always have a happy ending. Mystery readers believe that justice *should* be done, even if many crimes remain unsolved. Similarly, romance readers believe in the *possibility* of love capable of lasing a lifetime, while aware it will always take courage, self-knowledge, and consistent effort from both parties.

Did traditional fairy tales persuade every girl she was going to marry a prince?

Snow White, Sleeping Beauty, the Beast's Beauty and Cinderella have also been subjected to feminist criticism and revisionist versions. But these venerable tales are open to other interpretations. Snow White, cast out from her home and into danger, escaped and found friends among other outcasts from society. With generosity, goodness of heart and hard work, she ultimately earned her prince and his palace, no doubt with dozens of servants to do the housework.

Cinderella was also a worker, deprived of her rights and persecuted, who seized her opportunity when it was given, danced with the smitten prince long enough to persuade him no other woman had such character and charm, and the rest is fairy-tale history.

Sleeping Beauty disobeyed her father, the king (representing patriarchal society?), to experiment with forbidden technology, yet escaped death. Although the result of her curiosity put her life on hold, she remained inaccessible to inferior men until the most determined and suitable one came along to gently awaken her to the reward for her boldness—a new and happy life. Not a bad message for young girls tempted to experiment with the first randy teenager who pressures them for sex, risking not only disappointment but more serious consequences. Waiting for the right one paid off in the end for this princess. And the other Beauty learned that appearances may be deceptive; outward ugliness can disguise a true prince.

These themes are still used today under the guise of modern romance, no more likely to be taken literally than in their original form, but still passing on age-old female wisdom to new generations of women.

ROMANCE'S LONG HISTORY

The first English magazine for women, *Ladies' Mercury* (1693), addressed 'questions concerning love, marriage, behaviour, dress, and humour of the female sex'. The editor of *The Female Tatler* (1709) conceded that marriage for women was vital to social and economic survival, and set out to advise them on what sort of man was good husband material.

For eighteenth-century popular novelists like Mrs Eliza Haywood (*Love in Excess*) and Mary Davy (*The Reformed Coquet*), even daring to put pen to paper was in itself to engage in a feminist action. Education for females was frowned upon, and 'scribbling females' were disdained and derided by gentlemen who'd had the benefit of the schooling denied to women.

Periodicals such as *Records of Love* read like True Confessions of their time. Their stories reminded middle- and servant-class girls of the consequences of losing their 'virtue' to some seducer who would escape unscathed while she was 'ruinned' (*sic*), rendered unfit for marriage and perhaps even cast out on the streets by her family or employer. Other themes, such as Love Conquers All or True Love Will Find a Way, offered a subversive hope to rebellious young women subject to arranged marriages and fathers who gave 'advice to a daughter' to patiently submit to the husband chosen for her even if he were unfaithful, ill-humoured, miserly or feeble-minded (the Marquis of Halifax in *Ladies' New Year Gift*, published in 1700). Can we doubt the young ladies so addressed were grateful to be presented with this New Year gift by their menfolk?

The underlying nature of the literature of the ladies did not go wholly unnoticed. In 1864, Justin McCarthy, writing in the *Westminster Review* (vol. 82), pointed out that popular women novelists were prone to disposing of inconvenient husbands by way of divorce, desertion and suspicious deaths. It is difficult to determine if life imitated art or the other way around. In 1858 the British government had passed an act to regulate the sale of arsenic, and in 1860 a further act to restrict and regulate the sale of poisons, aimed at curtailing access to a favourite remedy used by discontented wives to rid themselves of household pests.

In 1858 women were granted a right to divorce, which you might think would have made such drastic solutions as rat poison unnecessary. However, while men could divorce their wives for adultery alone, women had to prove also a husband's physical cruelty, incest, rape, sodomy, bestiality, bigamy or two years' desertion. The legislation gave women control over money from bequests and investments, but not their own wages, possessions or capital—nor over their children. It was 1923 before they could sue for divorce on the same grounds as men, though few could afford to do so until a further amendment in 1937 made it less expensive.

Meanwhile Mrs Henry Wood (born Ellen Price) had published *East Lynne* (1861), a runaway bestseller followed by others, with sales of over two and a half million by 1900. The 'bits of religion' which rival novelist Charlotte Riddell accused her of 'throwing in . . . to slip her fodder down the public throat' and the dire consequences that beset *East Lynne*'s runaway wife allowed the book past the strict censorship of Mudie's famous lending library.

Modern feminist commentators with twenty–twenty hindsight have expressed disappointment in what they see as a failure of eighteenth- and nineteenth-century women writers to follow through the feminist agenda and overtly attack an oppressive society.

Remember that men governed the printing presses as they did women, and remember also the all-too-real penalties if a woman slipped from grace in the context of these authors' times. Lifelong disgrace, ostracism, shotgun marriages, perhaps being disowned by family, condemned to life on the streets or in the workhouse, an institution that survived into the 1930s.

Women who gained independence and maintained some respect were rare. Florence Nightingale was over thirty before she gained her father's permission to train as a nurse. Female adventurers like Lady Mary Wortley Montague, Lady Hester Stanhope and the Princess de La Tour d'Auvergne were of the aristocracy, who could afford to thumb their noses at the moralising of lesser mortals. Even so, Stanhope's lifelong sojourn in Egypt was said to have been a result of the scandal surrounding her taking a Scottish nobleman as her lover and travelling companion.

For the so-called 'sensation novelists', rewarding their heroines who flouted convention, family and religion would have been beyond even their extremely fertile imaginations. Bigamy, mysterious disappearances and murders, impersonations, hidden heirs, abductions, dastardly deeds and things that go bump in the night were far more easily conceived of than a future of equal rights, miniskirts and female prime ministers.

A slew of women writers paid lip service to the importance of virtue by having their heroines punished for its loss, while shining an accusing light on the dissatisfaction, injustice and resentments that festered beneath Victorian respectability. Their fallen women often evoked sympathy and even envy.

Mrs Wood describes the widowed Charlotte Pain in *The Shadow of Ashlydyat* (1863):

Having worn weeds for her husband, Charlotte emerged from her widowhood gayer than before. She rode more horses, she kept more dogs, she astonished . . . with her extraordinary modes of attire, she was altogether 'faster' than ever . . . . She held her court, she gave entertainments; she visited on her own score. Rumour went that Mrs. Pain had been left very well off . . . was popular in the neighbourhood . . . with the ladies as well as with the gentlemen . . . .

Charlotte was one . . . who did as she pleased . . . setting custom and opinion at defiance.

Retribution may be waiting in the wings, but meantime Charlotte is obviously having a high old time, and no doubt many readers indulged in some wishful thinking.

George Eliot (actually Mary Ann (Marian) Evans) was scathing of her less famous contemporaries, noting in a *Westminster Review* article (vol. 66, 1856) that compared to the heroine of what she called 'silly novels by lady novelists', '. . . the men play a very subordinate part by her side.

'. . . the tedious husband dies in his bed requesting his wife . . . to marry the man she loves best.'

Exactly. Where else can we find heroines who take centre stage *and* get what they want in the end? While Eliot defied society in her own life she seems to have missed the point here. More conventional women were quite capable of discerning the subtext behind the pious trimmings. In 1867 Margaret Oliphant opined:

> What is held up to us as the story of the feminine soul as it really exists underneath its conventional coverings is a very fleshy and unlovely record. Women driven wild with love for the man who leads them on to desperation . . . who marry their grooms in fits of sensual passion; women who pray their lovers to carry them off from husbands and homes they hate . . .

Mrs Oliphant—who, like Mrs Wood's heroine Charlotte—was widowed after four years (with three children, and another expected), may have suffered some professional jealousy of her racier sisters. She herself wrote on domestic relations with a certain acerbity. In *A Primrose Path* Mrs Bellingham opines: 'Fiddle-faddling eternally in the drawing-room, always in a woman's way wherever she turns. No, my dear, whoever you marry, Margaret, don't marry a clergyman; a man like that always purring about the fireside would drive me mad in a month.'

And she surely shows some dissatisfaction with the female role when in *Within the Precincts* a young man about to embark on a night out while his sister sits at home leaves her with the comforting thought that: '. . . you are a girl and girls are used to it . . . It's nature, I suppose. There isn't any fun for girls, as there is for us. Well, is there?'

Well, is there? Generations of girls have enjoyed romance novels that present them with more attractive and less obtuse men than this one. And many writers have slyly given their readers a wry smile or outright laugh at the expense of the male protagonist. A friend of mine who writes about men at the extreme end of the tough, gun-toting hero fighting for truth, justice and the heroine's love, delights in giving them embarrassing and very funny marshmallow moments.

The bewilderment and denial of an indestructible man felled by falling in love is a huge source of fun for romance readers. Susan Elizabeth Phillips's outrageously swollen-headed hero of *Heaven, Texas* (Avon Romance, 1995) is a prime example of a macho man struggling to escape the inevitable. Having boasted that from puberty he'd been pretty much of 'a stallion', when she leaves him he remembers that:

> The thing he appreciated about Grace was that she understood she wasn't really his kind of woman. She'd never make a scene about how she loved him and expected him to love her back, because she was realistic enough to know it wouldn't ever happen.
>
> Perversely, her acceptance now irritated him.
>
> . . . He was Bobby Tom Denton, for chrissake! Why was he letting her get to him like this? He was the one who held all the aces.
>
> That reminder should have calmed him down, but it didn't. Somehow or another, her good opinion had become important to him, because she knew him a lot better than anybody else he could think of off the top of his head. That realisation left him with a sense of vulnerability that was suddenly unbearable.

How the high-and-mighty are fallen!

Sandra Marton, who freely characterises her Harlequin Presents novels as pure fantasy, writes darker heroes in the Heathcliff tradition, but they too are frequently in denial about their real feelings. Dante, in *The Sicilian's Christmas Bride* (Harlequin Presents, 2006), ruminates:

He'd lost her through his own callous behaviour. He understood that now . . .

As recently as a few weeks ago, he'd still been lying to himself about his feelings for her. That whole thing about wanting to sleep with her to get revenge, get her out of his system . . .

Sheer, unadulterated lunacy.

It had always been easier to pretend she was just another woman passing through his life than admit his Tally was special. That what he felt for her was special. That what he felt for her was—that it was—

'Dante?'

No doubt relieved at the interruption, Dante still refuses to admit the word 'love' to his vocabulary for several more chapters. Marton's heroes are just the sort that have some militant feminists gnashing their teeth, because they just *don't get it*.

But millions of their sisters do. Men want to conquer mountains. Women want to conquer one man. And the bigger and badder he is, the more satisfying the victory. How many people would buy a book about climbing the Netherlands' 300-metre highest point at Valkenberg? Yet, numerous books have been written and read about the conquest of Everest (8800 metres and still growing). Similarly, a book about a nice girl who marries an amiable, housebroken specimen of the male species is about as exciting as a coddled egg.

THE CORE OF ROMANCE

Fighting isn't a necessary component of romance, but tension is. The most even-tempered hero can show a steely streak, or have his moments of quiet and terrifying anger. Whenever one of Betty Neels's large, sleepy-eyed doctor heroes spoke in a 'silken' tone, it sent shivers down my spine. Neels's impeccably written sex-free books had a huge following and are still being reprinted. Whether there is no sex on the page or explicit sex is a major component, the true core of romance speaks loud and clear to its target audience.

It's about women and *power*. In real life most women would likely run a mile from some of the hard men depicted (as the average man with any sense of self-preservation would from Goldfinger or Darth Vader), but in their chosen genre the stories are a delicious read.

Mary Burchell, writing for Mills & Boon between the 1930s and the 1960s, was quite pitiless towards her heroes, who took their power and privilege for granted until it hit them that some mousy girl had them in thrall. Typically, Burchell's heroes are lofty, superior and frequently impatient beings, like Quentin Otway in *Damaged Angel* (1966) who, finally laid low by love, admits to being 'ungenerous and unworthy', or Oliver who, in *Except My Love* (1937), realises 'he'd been so stupid, so lacking in understanding'.

> '. . . all the way home . . . I tried to imagine ways of telling you how sorry I was, but of course they didn't come very easily to me in those days.'
> 'He imagines they do now,' thought Erica amusedly.

Obviously Erica has the upper hand now, and is having a quiet laugh at Oliver's expense. Burchell's heroes at this point are often literally on their knees, described as boyish or childish, while the heroines embrace, reassure and mother them before allowing them to return to being masterful lovers. Few writers have so clearly invoked the fantasy at the heart of the genre.

The man the heroine wants for her lifelong companion, the father of her children, must be both strong and sensitive, and make her the centre of his world, the one person he will bow to.

Romance addresses needs, desires and concerns shared by women all over the world—choosing a mate, nurturing relationships, the preservation of our species, and women's place in the world. Ever-evolving, it changes as new challenges arise for women and as society alters its mores and its views. Young women today don't remember, as their mothers and grandmothers do, how men were allowed and even *expected* to behave, way back when. The romantic heroes of the last century were not greatly exaggerated examples of their sex at the time they were written.

Contemporary romance always takes place in the Now, and has often been in the vanguard of feminist thought. In a world where men ruled, heroines loyal to their own principles asserted their independence rather than succumb to the dictates of the men they loved.

LIBERATED SEX

For years before the new feminist wave of women's liberation, Mills & Boon writers like Mary Burchell, Eleanor Farnes and Rosalind Brett depicted young women struggling with the tension between careers and marriage. When IVF and surrogate motherhood came along, romance writers immediately began writing about the possibilities and pitfalls of the new technology.

In the seventies, romance writers liberated sex for their characters, and in the eighties there was a rash of books about single women finding real love with men who actually liked kids.

In 1996 Stephanie Herman noted in a cutting essay in *Women's Quarterly* that the contemporary feminist novel:

> . . . does not entail something that might make for good reading.
>
> . . . authors continually placed their female protagonists in situations where outside forces act upon them . . .
>
> Admittedly, these inert characters do survive— much as a slouching student in a back-row desk survives first period without being asked for the correct answer.
>
> . . . [merely] . . . surviving in a man's world is as essential to the modern feminist plotline as living happily ever after is to a Harlequin romance.

No surprise, then, that readers dissatisfied with literary fiction prefer the heroines of romance, who fight for the right to make their own choices, to shape their own lives and be recognised as equals or better by their men. Even so, the thought of a strong, protective partner available when needed is a welcome if wistful daydream for overburdened women.

Defined as escapist and meant for enjoyment, romance is not wholly light reading. My editors at Mills & Boon were a little nervous when I proposed a book about a woman who had been gang-raped and was unable to make love with her new husband. (It was suggested 'the feeling in the office is that she might have been only *nearly* raped'.) So I wrote the scene in which she finally tells the hero what happened, and M&B relented (*The Loving Trap*, 1980). I don't think any reader complained.

In a present-day setting the hero would have to be truly thick not to make a pretty good guess at the problem. That was when rape victims were shamed, and routinely accused in court of 'asking for it' if they wore a short skirt or deep neckline.

When another of my heroines committed adultery, however (*Marriage Under Fire*, Mills & Boon, 1983), there was a lot of outrage. I had ruined the fantasy with a scenario perhaps too close to home. In any other genre it would hardly have created a ripple. One irate reader spelled it out—she did not expect that kind of realism *in her romance reading*. I perfectly understood, but I also received more compliments for that book than any other. And I discovered recently via the internet that my Silhouette Intimate Moments (written as Laurey Bright) *A Perfect Marriage* (1995), in which the married hero cheats on the heroine, is still discussed among readers. In 2008 this book was included on the *Romantic Times* magazine readers' list of the 1001 best romances of all time.

PUSHING THE ENVELOPE

Somehow I gained a reputation for 'pushing the envelope' but it isn't something I ever deliberately set out to do. I write about things that interest me, hoping other women too would find interesting a love story dealing with that subject as part of the plot—as others before me had always done.

Romance writers decades ago covered subjects such as discrimination in the workplace and the home, and breaking out of women's narrow, defined roles. They have written about rape, incest, domestic violence, divorce and widowhood and troubled marriages, alcohol and drug addiction, child abuse, mental illness, anorexia, breast cancer, adoption, step-mothering, about mothers and teachers of special needs children or children in trouble—anything which affects women's lives. And sometimes we have written a traditional fairy tale with modern trimmings. Or simply put a new twist on an old story. Because that's what we do: tell stories. The primary requirement of any novel is that it tells a damn good story.

Many women writers in every age would have denied they were feminists. The medium, in this case the writer, *was* the message in a very literal sense. In the past they may have written about the problem rather than the solution. They wrote about women's lives, women's dilemmas, women's yearnings. Things that mattered to their sex.

But they wrote primarily to entertain their readers.

That is the function of the novelist, including those who write deeply literary analyses of the human condition, or misery novels about awful childhoods, or horror fiction, forensic procedurals, even thrillers about highly imaginative serial killers, with no detail spared. All these fantasies are highly popular. And all are outsold by romance. Which may be a source of relief to some of us.

Few writers can pull off polemical novels like those of Ayn Rand. Fiction can certainly contain life lessons, and many romance writers receive letters from readers who have learned something important, or have found hope and comfort in a particular story. It is highly dangerous, though, to set out to write a message rather than a story. Readers don't like being preached to. They will resent any effort to tell them how to live their lives. Frankly, I feel it would be colossal cheek, as well as a ludicrous proposition.

What a reader wants from romance is believable characterisation, an interesting plot, sexual tension (even if it's muted and any actual sex is off the page), and the emotional satisfaction of a great love story.

Falling in love is one of the nicest things in human experience, and reading about it is the primary pleasure of the genre.

If you want to write romance, remember that a woman who picks up your book wants just that—romance. While she may enjoy a thought-provoking theme, an exploration of a particular problem facing women in this post-liberation century, or an insightful study of a difficult relationship, she does not want to feel that the author is trying to tell her something—other than a good love story.

Every good romance has a heroine who is—or becomes by the end of the book—her own person, not to be pushed around by any male, even one she loves. She is aware of her own value, and able to stand up to anyone, including the hero, no matter how rich, successful or apparently superior he is. This applied equally to outwardly meek heroines of the thirties and forties and feisty corporate businesswomen of the seventies and eighties, and still applies now to the women of the new century who are able to take their rights for granted—until they come up against something to make them realise that despite many battles won, the war is not yet over.

Characters sometimes echo the writer's thoughts, but they are not mere vehicles for the writer's opinions. The story you want to tell and the characters you create arise from your subconscious. Your deepest beliefs become a subtle thread invisibly woven through everything you write.

BECAUSE YOU WRITE

Characters don't always behave as you would yourself. They may do things that you don't expect, that perhaps even shock you. It happens. *Because you are a writer*.

While writing *Fetters of the Past* (Laurey Bright, Silhouette Intimate Moments, 1985), I agonised for days trying to move the story on. While I knew they wanted to go to bed together, I was reluctant to have my protagonists' first lovemaking be a casual thing. At last I realised that my characters were less straitlaced than I was. Sleeping together was the logical next step. I went where the story wanted to go, and as it turned out, becoming lovers further complicated their relationship and made a more interesting book.

If your writing is any good these words on paper will take on life, will become people reacting in their own ways to the events you have created. And they will deal with the consequences in their own way, with some help from the writer.

What if your independent mover-and-shaker heroine is weeping inconsolably on the hero's shoulder? Or your sensitive new-age hero has sunk all his equal opportunity principles and overnight become a reactionary male chauvinist consumed by jealous rage?

Congratulate yourself. Your characters are real. They have faults and weaknesses just like you and me. They need to grow and change and understand themselves and each other, and something about the world they live in, so you can send them on the way to their happy ending. Or even just a positive, forward-thinking one. Wedding bells and happily-ever-after aren't obligatory, but *hope* is. And some kind of commitment to a future together.

Your readers may have important responsibilities; they may be overworked and under stress, whether with children or elderly parents to care for, or in a dead-end job or a high-flying career (perhaps more than one of these), and they may be alone. They understand how your fictional woman feels, and rejoice or perhaps envy that she is lucky enough to have a man around who understands—at least enough to offer comfort. And readers also understand that men, too, can be overwhelmed by their emotions, and not always the most admirable ones.

Characters acting against their own self-interest, their perceived goals or their avowed principles are characters in conflict with themselves, and that's the strongest conflict there is, making for a solid, interesting story-line.

Readers may be attracted to authors whose underlying views accord with theirs. Or even the most ardent feminist may want a total retro fantasy where men are *men* and women are willing to let them do the hard stuff. After all, it's good for their fragile male egos, and if there's a bear on the loose and a man willing to deal with it, what sensible female is going to volunteer? Make for the nearest tree!

Romance is not the enemy of feminism. It has a long and honourable history of informing, celebrating and, most of all, entertaining women, whoever and wherever they are. That's something its writers can be proud of as they continue a uniquely female tradition.

DAPHNE CLAIR is a New Zealander who decided that she wanted to be a writer after winning a school essay contest at eight years old and realising that there were people who earned a living writing stories. She has written almost seventy romance novels, mainly for Harlequin lines, a New Zealand historical novel as Daphne de Jong, and many poems, articles and short stories. She has won literary prizes, including the prestigious Bank of New Zealand Katherine Mansfield short story prize, and her romances have been praised by feminist critics. You can find out more about Daphne by visiting her writing class at www.daphneclair.com.

11

A FOOLPROOF
editing system

JENNIE ADAMS

We all face a range of challenges, whether from a busy and demanding home life, the constraints of an outside job, our need to meet editorial requirements, or all of the above. Helping ourselves get ahead of the game during stressful times can mean the difference between sinking or swimming. I definitely prefer to swim!

In today's writing climate, published authors can expect deadlines that must be met and revision requests on the majority of their books, no matter what area you write in: category romance, single title or specialist sub-genre. (I've always wanted to write an edgy story with strong fantasy elements. Do you think there'd be a market for my physically and psychically enhanced vampire hero from a special religious order that holds the world's salvation and survival in its hands?) *Anyway*, whatever you write or want to write, being able to meet deadlines and turn revisions around efficiently and effectively are vital to a successful ongoing career.

If publication (or continued publication) is your goal, it's important you're able to produce, polish and rework books not once, but consistently and repeatedly.

But all published authors manage their careers without struggles, right? Before I sold my first novel, I used to think so. Well, I'm going to tell you a story about how that isn't quite an accurate outlook, even when life is going well . . .

About a year ago my life was in a very manageable place. Family life was running smoothly, I was in good health, hubby was in good health, I was handling a part-time day job and my writing load and felt I could take on more. It was the perfect time to make a push to get further ahead with my writing career. I asked my editor for extra projects. Because she is wonderful and supportive and has invested in helping me forge ahead, and she too felt I was ready, I got those extra projects, which came close to doubling my writing workload for the year. But manageably. I could do this. I'd set a goal; it was reachable. This was going to be good for my career and I'd made a smart choice in going after it.

Scroll forward a number of months and as I write this chapter on foolproof editing, I have been through one bout of surgery that took me out of the game for six weeks and impacted on my writing for almost three months. I am writing this chapter on my laptop with stitches in my leg from a second operation. One of my children is pushing through a punishing final-year study workload, another is trying to organise an honours year at university.

Then, a few short months ago, the third child filled me with indescribable joy by coming home to me after a separation that started at his birth twenty-seven years before. This last one is huge by anyone's standards. Right now I am experiencing an overload of joy and happiness the likes of which I've never encountered in my life. I've been running around like a mother who just found her son. I'm also a mother trying to help her other children complete their tertiary studies; a wife worried about her family's health; a worker at an outside job; an author of books; and a woman who's had quite enough of having bits taken out by doctors . . . and . . . and . . . and . . .

Are you seeing yourself in some of this? This journey called 'life' takes up a lot of our time, thoughts and emotional resources. Sometimes we are taken by surprise for one reason or another, and need a little help to find our way forward.

SURVIVING THE CHALLENGES

You may be wondering what this has to do with editing systems. The answer is quite a lot, because it has to do with surviving challenging times, or ordinary times when we simply need that little 'lift' to keep going, or doubt-filled times, or overloaded times, and still getting where we need to go with our writing.

A fellow author said she had worked hard for the book projects she had and she wasn't giving any of them up. This year I signed contracts to write more books than I had produced in a given timeframe before. Not a scary amount, I don't think. Three books and a novella in around a twelve-month period. I write fast when I apply myself. When I took on those projects I knew that, with dedication, I could achieve them.

Did I make a dumb decision by increasing my workload and stress at a time when I needed to be able to focus on family and still get the remainder of my work done? I don't think so. I made choices based on the facts before me. The sudden upending of 'life' as I knew it into what would become 'a new better, even happier phase of life as I would learn to know it' wasn't something I could have anticipated.

It might be happiness, it might be loss or some other life-altering event, but things like this, in one form or another, *will* happen to all writers at some point. How we deal with these unexpected 'left turns of life' is where the value of the foolproof editing system comes in to help us survive and not only keep writing, but also produce our best work.

Whatever stage of writing career you have reached, the foolproof editing system can help you. You may be writing your first story and asking yourself what techniques you can use to make your work the best it can be. Or perhaps you're so close to publication you can smell it, and you're looking for the extra edge that will lead to your story's acceptance. Or maybe you're contracted to write more books this year, and concerned about managing your workload, needing some fresh means of producing your best work in the available time frame.

The foolproof editing system can be used for anything from plotting your story tweaks, tightening, revising and refocusing to surviving the revision request from hell. In short, it can be used at any time in your writing process from conception to final changes requested by an editor.

For the purpose of this chapter I'm going to explore four scenarios in which this editing system can be of help.

Scenario one: Okay, gulp. Now I'm scared. How can I possibly get these revisions right?
This scenario drove me initially to figure out my foolproof editing system. To backtrack a little, before

I took on the extra projects, I sent my editor a long synopsis outlining a story I wanted to write. I cried when I wrote that synopsis. My editor cried when she read it. The story inspired both of us, it covered a sensitive topic that I knew hadn't been written about much before, and it was particularly meaningful to me at the time of writing it. I admit I was totally in love with this hero before the story even began. Okay, I confess I'm still a little in love with Jack Reid. The topic was male breast cancer, and the book was *To Love and To Cherish* (Harlequin Romance, 2008).

Perhaps because I needed to dig into a very deep place emotionally, I found the story difficult to write. I did my best but, in the end, that best didn't do justice to the story premise. When my editor sent her revisions for the book, I realised I'd created a 'gentle landscape with a sun sinking slowly in the background'. What was needed was 'a ball of orange fire in the centre of the painting with everything else fanning out from it'. These are not my editor's words, but how I saw the situation.

There were so many changes necessary to get that manuscript up to scratch. Some of the requested revisions were major, changing overall aspects of the story that would flow through from the opening line to the ending. I also needed to make some changes to specific story elements, change various things on pages 27, 139 and . . . well, you get the idea. If the story hadn't touched both our hearts, maybe my editor would have given up on it before she nutted out those revisions. Maybe *I* would have given up when I saw the size and complexity of what she wanted, with no idea how I could pull the task off.

In the past I had handled revisions by reading my editor's revision letter until I felt certain I understood what was wanted, opening the manuscript document and 'having at it'. That's reasonably doable if the revisions aren't too complex. It wasn't going to work this time.

I panicked just a little when the revision request began to truly sink in. Okay, I admit I felt sick to the stomach and I remember buying a carton of cans of caffeine-loaded soft drinks, a family-sized block of chocolate, and lollies and other junk food in the quantities one might lay in for, say, an epic siege where survival was not guaranteed. This gives you an idea of my mindset at that point.

Nevertheless, I started to think about how I could tackle the revisions without making my head explode, or losing track of what needed to be done. There had to be some way to make so many diverse changes work. Preferably one that didn't make an enormous mess of my manuscript document and result in a worse end product than when I started working on it.

At this point the thought crossed my mind that 'desperation must needs be the mother of figuring out how to make something work'. And from somewhere in my mind, I dredged out a memory that gave me a hint of what I needed to do.

In the movie *Dirty Dancing*, Johnny and a team of friends work each summer at a family holiday resort where they teach and demonstrate dance. Beautiful 1960s dances, like the merengue and the pachanga and, when they are not on display, dances they have created for their own entertainment and pleasure.

Johnny is a wonderful dancer. When his partner is in his arms, she is completely safe with him. He knows his material, knows his moves, and he can take her through the dance and make her look beautiful, polished and wonderful. The dance is totally in his control so it *looks* effortless, smooth and delightful. That's where we want our books to end up, even if we need to do major revisions to get there.

One day, Johnny explains to the heroine, Baby, how he learned his skills as a dance teacher and exhibitionist by breaking down each of the dances into its component moves, then piecing those moves back together. He built his own individual dance routines in the same way. Something about this explanation clicked with me when I first heard it. I thought Johnny looked rather nice without a shirt on, too, but that's another story.

As I thought about it, I figured if dances could be stripped down, put back together and perfected in this way, why not do the same with stories? In the end, stories are made up of components just as dances are. My editor had asked me to work on a variety of components in my revisions. If I broke down what I had into its components, maybe I could figure out how to put it back together stronger and better so the story would become what we wanted.

I stripped the story down into plot, action, emotion, romantic development, etc. I converted my editor's revision letter into a point-form list of what needed to be done. Then I played jigsaw puzzles with the elements until I figured out what was needed, and took that to the manuscript itself. I'll explain this process more fully in the second part of this chapter.

Scenario two: I've lost the plot. Literally. I'm on page 145 and I still don't know what this story is about.
This scenario happened to me with one of my books. I don't know why, but I couldn't connect with the characters and, because my stories come out of my characters, I wasn't getting into the creative zone with it. It didn't matter how much time I spent working on the story or reading over what I'd written, I just couldn't see what was missing.

I had my editing system in place when this situation occurred. I'd used it successfully on the revisions I described above. I decided, 'Why not use the system here, too?'

To resolve my 'part-way through the book and no idea where it's going' problem, I broke down what I had in the story to that point. Then I looked at the weak spots and built them up in summarised form.

I mixed and matched the results, looked at the remaining plot, built it up as well. And then I trusted the system to get me, if not all the way there, at least close to a publishable-standard story that I would be able to bring the rest of the way home. I still didn't know my characters at the end of that first draft, but I had a really strong foundation down for them and could finally tease them out, sprinkle that bit of 'magic dust' on them that comes from deep inside, and I had the materials already in place to allow that to work. It may not be an ideal writing process overall, but it got me there and, in the end, that's what counts.

Scenario three: My draft is okay but it needs depth.
This one comes into play with every single book I write. There are authors who write great first drafts and only have to go through once and polish up a bit. I don't really want to blow up their letterboxes.

I always need to improve on the draft. A lot. And the more books I write, the harder I find it to assess the work at draft level simply by reading through it and making changes. Though it does take time to outline what I have and assess it and improve on it, in the end it's a more effective means of working out what I still need to do to bring the story up to scratch.

Scenario four: I'm distracted beyond belief and I have deadlines. How do I even start a book in this state? Help!
Five months ago my eldest son and I were reunited in unusual circumstances that involved me being given the chance to truly be a mother to him when I had thought that opportunity denied to me for all time. This gift overwhelmed me with so many emotions, such joy and happiness, gratitude and love, that, for the very first time in my writing career, I hit a place where not only was I distracted, I was not sure I would ever be able to write a cohesive piece of fiction again.

That may sound a little overwrought now, but for several months I truly did experience that level of distraction. Who knew, for example, that you could read a manuscript out loud while standing up on a hard floor wearing uncomfortable shoes and drinking caffeine drinks to ensure an adequately sharp state of mind, and still *daydream the entire time and not take in a word you were reading, let alone comprehend what it was supposed to mean*?

I doubt there are many more lovely ways to be distracted. But I did effectively lose three months of writing time. Oh, I sat at the computer for hours on end most days. Sometimes I even got words onto the page, but I dredged those words out one by one,

I was so slow, I wasn't getting where I needed to be with the story, and what was a story all about again anyway? Something about characters and a plot? My concentration was a mess.

There will be times in life for all of us, I suspect, when we simply *can't* write. If you are in that place because of great joy or terrible grief or any other reason, be kind to yourself and take the time out that you need. If you are able to forge on, a solid editing system can help you through.

During this distracted time in my life, I turned to my editing system to help me. I finished my current book project about two weeks after it was due. I wasn't entirely satisfied with it but, by using my editing system, I got as close as I could.

When I received the revisions for that story, they were quite doable I'm happy to say. The story reached far more of its potential than it would have otherwise, thanks to my being able to look at its components and see what I needed to work on before I submitted it. Using the system again as I work on the revisions will help me to get them done quickly and effectively.

So, plotter or pantser, whether you like to lay out a story in linear fashion before you type the first word in your manuscript, or dive into chapter one with no idea where this wild ride will take you, there will be times when taking things back to basic 'dance moves' in your story will help you to work faster, fix a problem, and achieve a stronger overall result. Or simply keep going.

THE FOOLPROOF EDITING SYSTEM

Consider the components that make up your story. You defined these initially by reading editorial guidelines for your target market, studying current books published within that line by your chosen publisher, and considering the personal core themes and elements that you would write into each of your books.

Bear in mind these will vary depending on what kind of story you write. My books are short category romances of 50000–55000 words focusing on the emotional journey of the hero and heroine, and the developing romance between them. One of my personal core themes is family, so that makes its way into my list as well. You might have sub-plots that support your main plot or run parallel to it, or a sub-genre element such as mystery, paranormal or suspense. Whatever those elements are, you can include each one in your break-up, as I do.

For the purpose of this example, I will keep things relatively simple and define my story components as follows:

1. Story progress—what's actually happening in action in each scene.

2. Heroine's internal conflict—what's stopping her from acting on her attraction to the hero.
3. Hero's internal conflict—what's stopping him from acting on his attraction to the heroine.
4. Heroine's romantic development.
5. Hero's romantic development.
6. Other story elements.

1. Story progress

What action takes place to move the story forward, and where does it happen? When you record your story progress for this purpose, include the scene setting and remember your international readership. Ask yourself the questions, 'How can the story action strengthen the story or support other elements of it?' and 'How can I use setting to add to the mood, suspense, romance, conflict or overall appeal for the reader?'

Setting can present opportunities for interesting scene twists, so don't be scared to experiment. In *To Love and To Cherish*, a scene I had a lot of fun with involved the heroine chasing a goat across a paddock with a portable milking machine. Using this scene led to a terrific one–two punch of humour and heartache that drew the reader deep into the heroine's hurts, and lent great empathy for her. The scene came up because I decided I wanted to set some of the story on a goat farm and googled milking methods.

2. Heroine's internal conflict

The heroine's internal conflict needs to progress arm in arm with the development of her romantic feelings towards the hero. How can you progress this story arc? Lend the most emotional strength to it? I have an unwelcome habit of going in circles in this area. Laying the conflict out using my editing system allows me to ensure a feasible forward progression.

3. Hero's internal conflict

Isn't it fun to torture our heroes? We writers are ghoulish creatures really. It's just as much fun in real life but don't tell anyone I said that.

When torturing your hero—I mean, *when working on his internal conflict*—look for ways to make him the man all of us would fall in love with. He can be as tough as he likes, provided we see the chinks in his armour that will eventually have him on his knees to his heroine, heart in hand for her. Told you I'm ghoulish!

Let your hero believe he's in complete control until the next disaster strikes, usually as the result of the heroine somehow outsmarting his efforts at that control. The stakes and the conflict escalate once again!

4. & 5. Heroine and hero's romantic development

I adore this part. The curiosity, the interest, the drawing close and pushing apart. Oh, the agony and joy and desperation and excitement! Pile it on, make it real. Imbue your characters with feelings we all know and understand, and, where you can, *show don't tell*, let us see what's happening rather than tell us. For example, rather than telling the reader that your heroine is determined and doesn't give up easily, show her chasing a goat across a paddock with a portable milking machine!

An example of expressing the romantic development comes from my first Harlequin Romance, *The Boss's Convenient Bride* (Harlequin Mills & Boon Romance, 2005). My heroine, Claire, is in her boss Nicholas's office prepared to take dictation from him. Instead, she gets the impression he is asking her to vet candidates for matrimony. As Claire has something of a crush on her boss herself, she's not particularly happy at this thought but she doesn't want to reveal her feelings:

'We'll find someone appropriate for you, don't worry.' Claire could do this. It wasn't as if she *really* cared about Nicholas.

'I've already found her.'

Claire's pencil drew a deep, squiggly line across the page and tore through to the pages below. She forced her hand to stop, and looked up, feigning a calm expression she didn't feel. 'You have?'

We see what Claire is thinking quite clearly, although the hero doesn't at this point.

6. *Other story elements*

Whatever your other elements, you will be able to work out how to use them to greatest advantage as you think about your work at this 'dance moves' level.

Once you have your story components listed, allocate a coloured paper or highlighter pen to each component. For the purpose of this example I suggest using the following colours:

1. Story progress—green.
2. Heroine's internal conflict—yellow.
3. Hero's internal conflict—orange.
4. Heroine's romantic development—pink.
5. Hero's romantic development—blue.
6. Other story elements—purple.

Okay, I confess I chose these colours because they were all easily obtainable by me. Hint: find the coloured paper *first* and then allocate your colour choices, or, if you're using white paper and coloured highlighters, choose the highlighters first.

The next step is to summarise the development of each of these components. What is wanted at this stage is the briefest summary possible, in point form for ease of readability. If you're plotting your story from scratch, ask yourself the kinds of questions I've outlined in the above explanations. Colour code the results using paper or highlighters, lay everything out on the floor or your dining table, then look at what you have and search out the weak spots.

Do you have three chapters with no pink or yellow? That may mean you aren't getting to know your heroine sufficiently, or you're giving the hero's conflict and development a little too much space in those chapters.

Ask yourself, 'Does each story component follow an arc that progresses and makes sense for the story? Do all the components work together to give the hero and heroine lots of ghoulish pain and suffering before they reach a wonderfully satisfying resolution at the end of the story?'

If you're part-way through writing your story and feeling lost, do the same thing. Once you have everything laid out, you'll be able to see the weak spots and sort out what needs to be done to get you on track and you'll give yourself the opportunity to work on your components one at a time, even if you can't yet get your head around the overall story picture.

Use the same methodology for polishing strength into your draft.

This is a breakdown of the first chapter of my third published Harlequin Romance, *Her Millionaire Boss*:

1. Heroine at hospital guarding elderly boss (green).
2. Altercation with boss's wife. First hint heroine's internal conflict. She won't abandon boss (yellow).
3. Hero arrives, inspires her curiosity and interest (pink).
4. Hero is grandson who abandoned her boss. Heroine has big issues with abandonment! (yellow).
5. Hero tormented about leaving his grandfather. Hint at his internal conflict but not all explained (orange).
6. Hero attracted to heroine, who has preconceived dislike of him (blue).
7. Leave hospital together, forced into working relationship for good of grandfather (purple).

Questions to ask yourself about your components:

- Does each story component move the thread forward, reaching the strongest conclusion and covering all possible useful story ground in the process? If not, add in what you feel is missing.
- Are all components in balance for the target market? For example, if writing for a market that is heroine focused, her conflict arc may receive more space than that of the hero, or the hero's

conflict arc may be represented through the heroine's eyes (point of view), not his.

Revisions and jigsaw puzzle time:

- For revisions or for times when you discover you not only need to improve on what you have, but you need to shuffle elements, or make big changes, take your pieces of coloured paper to your dining table or clear some floor space. Lay it all out as it appears in the story now, plus the additions you made when you examined the arc of each separate element. Now, what can you see yet again that could do with being strengthened for the sake of the overall story? Make those changes.
- Is your story in the right order? Maybe you've realised something that happens in chapter seven should have occurred a lot sooner. This is your opportunity to shuffle the story development to best suit your needs. Doing this with coloured pieces of paper or highlighters while your manuscript document sits safe and sound on the computer is very freeing. There is no need to worry that you might make a mess or do something too drastic. It's just paper. You can shuffle as many times as you like until you're sure that what you've done will work.

- Once you're satisfied you have everything in order, all components as strong as possible, pin your coloured pieces of paper in order on a cork board, open your manuscript document (and save it as a different file name) and you're ready to start making your improvements.

- You will find you can turn big revisions around faster and more effectively by breaking down your story components and incorporating your revision changes first at this level. The same rule applies to refocusing a story. This is much easier to do at summary level first.

It is very easy to over-revise a story if you don't employ some means of controlling what you change in the manuscript. By outlining your story's elements and the changes you intend to make, you will ensure that you hold on to all the wonderful aspects of your story that don't need changing at all!

Good luck, and I hope to see your edited, shining, dance-steps-perfected work on the shelves the next time I'm browsing for a fabulous romance novel that flows together so effortlessly and looks so beautiful on the dance floor (I mean on the *page*) that no one would believe it all came together with the help of a little bit of hard work, some coloured paper and a cork board, perhaps some junk food (if you're like this author) . . . and a foolproof editing system.

JENNIE ADAMS lives in inland New South Wales, and is the proud mother of three amazing adult children. One of Jennie's long-term dreams was to write romance novels for readers around the world, and she takes great pleasure in the fulfilment of that dream. She recently sold her tenth romance novel to Harlequin, and won a 2009 Romantic Times award for *The Boss's Unconventional Assistant*. Her books have featured on the Waldenbooks USA bestseller list. The chance to contribute to a how-to book with fellow authors, sharing their real-life experiences of novel creation 'from the trenches', was too great for Jennie to pass up. Rather than 'craft expertise' Jennie refers to her writing tips as 'survival tactics'. To learn more about Jennie's work, please visit her website at www.jennieadams.net.

12

LIVING,
breathing characters

MULTI-FACETED PEOPLE

One day, in my local shopping mall, a toddler broke away from his mother and ran towards the travelator where a trolley collector pushing fifty shopping trolleys was coming the other way. The outcome, in about two seconds' time, would have been one squashed little boy. Near the top of the travelator was a big, tough man who, quite frankly, I wouldn't have wanted to meet in an alley at night. When he saw what was about to happen to the child, the man got a look of utter panic on his face. He dropped his 'tough' facade, and gently lifted the child to safety. Mother and son were reunited and I smiled as I watched this bear of a man blush and stammer as he accepted the woman's thanks.

Without that incident to bring out his 'other side' all I would have seen was a scary man. An insight into what was inside him made all the difference. When you write your characters, let them live and breathe all the sides of themselves. Let your tough guy character be a marshmallow about little children, your heroine forget where she parked her car or have a completely irrational fear of picking up food from a drive-through window (yes, this author is guilty as charged). Make your characters real, and watch your readers take those characters into their hearts— for keeps.

Jennie Adams

CREATE A REACTION

When we first start writing, we're told we must create three-dimensional characters. For me, the characters have to live, breathe, be a part of me before I write the book. I have to hear those characters talking to me in my head before I can even start writing. I see my characters as real people and hope I give them the same attributes as the people I meet in my daily life, warts and all. I want the reader to care what happens to these characters. Good, bad or indifferent, I want to create a reaction in the reader.

Alexis Fleming

THE SOUL OF THE STORY

In my view, without a multi-layered, three-dimensional story, all you have are words on a page. The reader wants to see the soul of the story, and it's up to the writer to provide this. Characters need to not only resemble real people, but also live and breathe on the page. This makes the story real, makes the reader think 'what if?'

As I write, I have a picture in my head of what my characters look like. I'll trawl the internet for pictures and I'll create a collage of their features. This way I actually have a clear image in front of me. I also make sure I give the characters quirks that make them more real. I chew my nails—why shouldn't my character as well?

Kelly Ethan

KEEPING CHARACTERS TOGETHER

I suspect that the classic romance hero is often wealthy because it's a way of keeping the characters together for more of the book. When I've written about a hero who works for a living, it's a challenge accounting for the time when the two are supposedly at work. Self-employed people generally have more flexibility, and bosses don't have to account for their time to others: possibly the reason why so many lone wolves, corporate stars and billionaires are cast as romantic heroes. It doesn't hurt the fantasy either.

Valerie Parv

THE RIGHT NAME

My main characters largely create themselves, I think. They walk into my mind and it's up to me to get to know them properly like any other acquaintance. Any characteristic or trait that I try to foist onto them for my own convenience, they usually shrug off. I discover who they are by writing about them. I nearly always end up writing useless scenes that have to be cut because they add nothing to the story. But they aren't entirely useless because that seems to be part of my 'writing in' process. They help me to write myself into the story and get to know the characters. I'll tell you one thing, though: characters don't come to life for me until they have a name. Not just any name— the right name.

Elizabeth Rolls

MEAT AND HEART

A common mistake is to equate being 'sympathetic' with being 'perfect'. Perfect characters are not sympathetic.

Perfect characters are namby-pamby goody-two-shoes who make readers want to throw up, or throw the book across the room. Sympathetic characters have flaws—real ones that the reader can identify with, that can make her wince or laugh or groan.

Let's not make the flaws too cute, either. Sometimes you can almost see the writer thinking, 'Ooh, better give her some flaws', and we end up with an uptight corporate lawyer who's suddenly a ditz around the photocopy machine for no apparent reason and it's . . . yeah, way too cute.

Character flaws have to have some meat and heart to them. They're not worn like a frivolous accessory. They come from deep inside, and are often the other side of the same coin that creates a character's talents and strengths. A committed artist never hears the phone ring, and constantly runs late for appointments and meetings. A high-powered executive doesn't know how to unwind. Even that lawyer who's a ditz with the photocopy machine . . . It turns out that, thanks to some important series of events in her past, she's learned to trust her mind but not her body. She freezes any time she has to use her hands, whether it's to make a pie, operate an unfamiliar car, or unbutton the hero's shirt. Not too cute, after all.

Lilian Darcy

PEOPLE-WATCHING

I love people-watching. I might be sitting in a café and I'll see an attractive girl who has something that makes her stand out—the way she walks or wears her clothes—and my imagination wanders. I start to wonder what she does for a living, if she has a boyfriend. Then I might see an attractive man and my creative juices flow. I put them together and build a life for them, a reason for meeting and a conflict, and go from there.

Helen Bianchin

LARGER THAN LIFE

Give your heroine a man who has the capacity to utterly love her, maybe in larger-than-life ways. Are you writing a romantic suspense? Then let him jeopardise his life to save hers, literally. Translation for the reader— this is a hero who will always do what needs to be done to ensure her wellbeing, even at great risk to himself.

Give her a flaw, and let him adore that about her. Maybe she's an awful cook but she tries really hard (read my book *The Boss's Unconventional Assistant* to check out this scenario). Give *him* a flaw. Perhaps he's a little too inclined to take charge. Let him try it, butt up against her resistance and be completely flummoxed by it. Suddenly we will all adore him because we can *see* his love for her is going to keep him twisted up in knots for the rest of his life, and this appeals because we too want to be loved, flaws and all, don't we?

Jennie Adams

REVEALING CLOTHES

Possessions, pets, cars, are all indications of character and outlook. Clothes reveal the wearer's taste, economic situation and how she feels about herself. Incidentally, don't put your protagonists in clothes likely to date them. Sketch secondary characters with a telling but brief phrase, let them do their bit to help the plot along, then have them disappear while you get back to the vital business of telling the story of your hero and heroine and their journey towards love.

Robyn Donald

WHAT DO YOU WANT?

A great way to bring characters to life for yourself is to ask them questions. Who are you? What do you want from life? What do you care about most? Hate the most? Fear the most? Let the answers come to you in whatever form they choose, without trying to force anything or edit the results.

At first the answers may come slowly, but if you stay with the process, they will gradually pick up pace until you're writing the answers at full speed. I learned this method from the late Gene Roddenberry, creator of the Star Trek universe, who used the process to create the logical Vulcan, Mr Spock. It wasn't metaphysical, Gene said, but merely a means of accessing information he already had in his mind, but buried below conscious recall.

Valerie Parv

13

ALL IN THE
point of view

GET INTO THE SANDPIT

Have you heard the saying 'There are three points of view—his, hers and the truth'? I once watched and listened unobserved from inside the house while my two youngest children played in the backyard sandpit. They got silly and giggly, having that little bit *too much* of a good time. The next thing I knew they were both covered from head to toe in sand. As I had a rule, 'No sand in the hair', I wondered what would happen when they came inside and had to face up to the 'Wrath of Mum'. Basically, it went like this:

Me: How did you both get sand all over you and in your hair?

Son: She doesn't like me and that's why it happened.

Daughter: He's bossy. He said I *had* to get sand on me and he made me *eat* sand, too.

Interesting. There'd been no sand eating. No bossing, no fighting. What I was told certainly weren't the facts as I had seen them. The children, perhaps trying to give their excuses more impact, took the story to an emotional level. So it needs to be with our characters. There are a lot of suggestions for using point of view, such as sticking to one point of view per scene or per chapter. Mine is to ask yourself which character's point of view lends the most strength to that part of the story, which takes it to the strongest emotional level. Sometimes my editor will ask me to switch viewpoint if she believes there could be more strength if I get into another character's head. Let the viewpoint character see events in their way, with their own slant on things. It's okay for their view to differ from reality. Life in the sandpit can be like that, too!

Jennie Adams

CATCH YOURSELF THINKING

Writing in viewpoint is simply about expressing how the character feels, but seen from within the character, rather than from outside. I practice this skill by 'catching myself thinking' during different emotional states. While this may sound self-conscious, it's a useful exercise in seeing life through a writer's eyes.

For example, next time you're exhausted, note how your body feels—are you perspiring, do your feet feel sore or even blistered, are your temples throbbing with the warning of a headache coming on? What's going on in your head? Are you longing for a cup of tea and a sit-down? Looking forward to curling up with a book, or indulging yourself with a dip in a hot tub? (Lucky you!) Or telling yourself how pleased you are that a dreaded chore is finally out of the way? These are the kinds of details you can give to your heroine when she's tired—so the reader experiences the feeling directly, rather than being told about it.

Valerie Parv

SHOULD YOU 'HEAD-HOP'?

Oh, boy, I am the world's worst when it comes to point of view. I wrote my first manuscript knowing nothing about the craft of writing. I just had characters inside my head who demanded their own story. I think I head-hopped (switched viewpoints) every second paragraph. The manuscript is still sitting in a box in my garden shed.

I've learned a lot since then, although I still break the rules a bit. Standard practice is one point of view per scene. However, for me, knowing what both characters are thinking and feeling enriches the story. So I quite often have both points of view in the one scene, but I always leave a line space to signify the change of point of view, and I start off the new section mentioning the character's name so the reader isn't confused. It doesn't work for everyone, but it's how my brain handles the task.

Alexis Fleming

WHEN AND WHY TO CHANGE

I'm not a purist here. I've heard the one-POV-per-scene rule, and the one-change-per-scene-if-you-must amendment, and I'm not fully convinced by either. I've enjoyed too many books where the POV changes with great frequency. The thing is to know why you are changing and to change the POV deliberately, and for a very good reason, rather than because your grip on whose psyche you were in wasn't strong enough. The benefit of POV is that it allows you and the reader to focus on a particular character. Sometimes flipping back and forth is just inexperience—and yes, been there, done that—got the book to prove it!

Elizabeth Rolls

DON'T SLOW THE ACTION

Switching point of view can enhance the story, but often it leads to a slackening of pace and tension. If the dual point of view doesn't add anything new to the movement of the plot or the reader's understanding of the characters, it's just slowing the action.

Many successful romances are still written entirely from the heroine's POV. A good rule of thumb if a switch seems necessary is: one scene, one POV. Then the reader is less likely to experience the ping-pong effect. And how do you indicate the hero's feelings if you never get inside his mind? Describe his telltale body language.

Giving the reader a God's-eye view places her outside the scene, no longer intimately sharing one person's emotions. Sometimes God's eye is useful for setting the scene at the start of the book or chapter, but otherwise it's usually best to be sitting on a character's shoulder or inside the character's emotion and thought throughout the story, rather than looking on from above.

Daphne Clair

EMOTIONAL INVOLVEMENT

One of the biggest traps in new writing is dabbling around the edges of emotional issues. This shows up most commonly in love scenes. If we feel uncomfortable writing so intimately about our characters, it's all too easy to slip into the omniscient viewpoint, writing, 'they did this . . .' and 'they did that . . .'. This immediately puts a distance between the writer and what the characters are experiencing, and the reader misses out on the emotional involvement.

Valerie Parv

CONTROLLING POINT OF VIEW

I think we sometimes try to be too specific and mechanical with 'the rules' about point of view. When I'm reading, I'll forgive an author switching points of view all over the place, even hopping without warning into an omniscient narrator's viewpoint, *as long as it doesn't pull me out of the story.*

I think this is the key. We object to sloppy point of view *because* it pulls us out of the story. We think, 'Hang on, who is thinking/seeing/feeling this?' or 'But how does *she* know he couldn't find the missing letter?', which means we've stopped our satisfying surrender to the flow of the story and have screeched on the brakes and put our heads into gear. When the writing is good enough, we don't even notice sloppy or inconsistent point of view. When the writing is flowing well enough, the author may not notice it either.

That said, I don't think 'flow' should be used as an excuse. As writers, we should try our utmost to be in control of point of view, and if something about the story isn't working, questioning the point of view we've used can lead to new solutions. We might realise that the emotional stakes would be higher if the reader was experiencing the scene from the hero's point of view, rather than the heroine's. Or that if we were deep enough inside the murderer's head, we'd know where the body was hidden, even without giving away to the reader which character's eyes we were seeing through.

Lilian Darcy

STAYING IN VIEWPOINT

Viewpoint characters spend so much time in front of mirrors and store windows because it's the only way the writer can tell us how they see themselves, while staying in viewpoint. If we're boiling mad, for example, we can't see ourselves turning red with anger unless we can see our reflection. However, we can feel the heat blooming on our skin, and our hands start to tremble, and this is what the writer should be describing.

A good way to test whether you are staying in viewpoint is to write a few paragraphs then read them aloud, substituting 'I' for 'she', and making any other small grammatical changes this requires. The passage should still sound plausible. If not, there may be places where you are slipping out of viewpoint, such as by having your character see her face turn red, or other giveaways.

Valerie Parv

SIGNAL THE READER

Transitions are notorious for producing padding. All you have to do to get your heroine from a pearl farm in Tahiti to New Zealand is allow two double lines of spacing and a new paragraph. But if she meets her hero on the plane and sparks fly, we want a scene with carefully chosen detail to act as signals to the reader. What your viewpoint character can see, hear, feel, smell and taste; the action cues that reveal her thoughts as opposed to what she's saying; the bits of business that reveal emotions she's trying to hide; these are important because they show the heightened state of her awareness of the hero.

Robyn Donald

14

SPEAKING

of dialogue

HIDDEN MEANINGS

Dialogue can say much more than the words on the page. People hide their feelings with speech as often as they reveal them. Romantic protagonists are often concealing a great deal from each other, but with the writer's help the reader will decode the hidden meaning behind what the characters say.

The hero says, sweeping the heroine with a disparaging glance, 'That dress might attract the wrong kind of attention.' To which the heroine replies, 'Maybe you're right. I hadn't expected you to bother speaking to me.'

You can reveal the characters' true feelings through their body language. The tightening muscle in his jaw, the tiny pulse beating in her throat, signal powerful emotions deliberately controlled. (And they are so effective that unfortunately both have been overused.) Breaks in dialogue during a dramatic conversation not only allow the reader a respite from unbroken passages of speech, or ensure she knows who has said what. They give the writer an opportunity to provide physical clues to the emotions—the subtext—driving the scene.

Daphne Clair

TRY READING ALOUD

Dialogue is usually where my scenes start in my head. They start with characters talking. One thing I have to watch is that my characters don't natter on too long for one speech. People don't usually make great long speeches without the other person nodding off. On the other hand lots of short, snappy dialogue creates lots of white space on the page, which may lead to page count problems depending on your publisher. You have to balance this. Try reading your dialogue aloud; act out your scenes. Remember that people have quite different ways of talking. Hate to say it, but women tend to talk more, give more detail. Men less so, unless prodded.

Elizabeth Rolls

THE WORK OF DIALOGUE

Writers generally fall into two camps—narrative writers and dialogue writers. I'm naturally a dialogue writer, and have to remember to slip in occasional bits of what playwrights call 'business'—the things the characters are doing while they're talking to each other. I find dialogue much more pacy and interesting than narrative, and far more enjoyable to write.

If you find dialogue hard to write it may help to remember the work the writing has to do. Dialogue isn't idle chatter to break up the narrative, it's a crucial part of the storytelling. Among the tasks dialogue has to do are: get reader's attention and set the story in motion; let the characters reveal themselves; provide information so the writer doesn't have to 'tell' the reader; add pace and tension; create emotion; move the story along.

Valerie Parv

WORDS WITH PUNCH

Dialogue represents the words our characters speak, but the words need to be the *right* words. There's a difference between the heroine saying, 'I really don't like you, Brad' compared to 'I wouldn't have you if you were the last man on Earth!'. The first version is rather bland, whereas the second example has some *punch*.

Helen Bianchin

PACE YOURSELF

Dialogue is an important part of pace; it's easy to read, inherently interesting and reveals character far better than straight narrative. Good dialogue should be convincing and colloquial. If in doubt, read your dialogue aloud, listening carefully for rhythm and vocabulary. Do the words reflect the character's background, age, sex, interests and emotions? Remember, truck drivers don't talk like lawyers. Ethnic groups have different ways of speaking. Men don't sound like women. Listen to what you've written, listen to the people around you, listen to your characters. Make sure that every incident, every careful description, every sexy conversation, or every long, heavy-lashed look, pushes the plot forward, reveals character and establishes setting and mood.

Robyn Donald

EMOTIONAL STATES

Coupled with narrative which allows the reader into the character's thoughts, dialogue can create an intriguing or revealing counter-impression.

'Ah, you look, ah—' Stunning, gorgeous, overwhelmingly male and powerful and compelling. All these words fitted. Soph settled for a lame, '—businesslike.'

The counter-impression tells us Soph (*The Boss's Unconventional Assistant*, Harlequin Romance, 2008) is very aware of the hero, but that she's trying hard not to let him see that. Dialogue can help express your characters' emotional state, even if what they are *saying* is quite the opposite.

Jennie Adams

ADDING TEXTURE

The *he said, she said* describe the tone and manner in which the hero and heroine speak, together with any facial expression, gestures etc. as and where the writer feels they add texture.

There are, of course, any number of words that convey *said*. Check out your thesaurus (Roget's is excellent), or key *said* into your computer thesaurus, then explore all the various synonyms, cross-referencing them to add to a knowledge base of *said*.

Helen Bianchin

BODY LANGUAGE

Okay, so you have a nice dialogue going, you've added the *he said* or *she said* tags . . . now you need to add in some body language and emotional reaction to describe what the hero or heroine is feeling, and also where they are in this particular scene.

Here is an example taken from *The Martinez Marriage Revenge*:

It would be so very easy to link her hands behind his neck and silently invite him to rekindle the flame.

And she almost did. *Almost.*

Except sanity and the dawning horror of where this was going provided the impetus to pull away.

What was she doing?

Was she out of her mind?

'I hate you.' The words came out as a tortured whisper as she dropped her arms and attempted to move back a pace.

For what seemed an age Marcello examined her features, the dilated eyes so dark, almost bruised, with passion. The soft, swollen mouth trembling from his possession.

The shocked dismay.

'Perhaps you hate yourself more,' he offered quietly.

For losing control? *Enjoying* his touch?

And, dear lord . . . wanting it all.

He watched as she straightened her shoulders, tilted her chin and summoned a fiery glare.

'I'm done. And *that*,' she flung recklessly, 'was a ridiculous experiment.'

Marcello let her go, watching as she moved towards the door and exited the room.

Experiment? Far from it.

A mark of intent.

And he was far from done.

Helen Bianchin

DISTINGUISHING QUIRKS

I think I work very intuitively in this area, perhaps because of my background in studying European languages and linguistics, and my writing for theatre and television. I tend to create a character, make them as real and three-dimensional and believable in my head as I possibly can, and then just turn them loose and listen to them speak.

I don't have to come up with distinguishing quirks, particular turns of phrase or voice tones, because they do that themselves. It's simply the way they speak. I realise this I'm-helpless-in-the-grip-of-my-muse approach might be really annoying for people who don't feel that they have an intuitive grasp of dialogue. On the down side, I think it makes my dialogue less flamboyant and exciting than that of many authors because the reality is that most people *don't* speak in a particularly original, clever and flavourful way. They say things like, 'Did you pick up the dry-cleaning?' and 'What's for dinner?' and 'Goodnight, everyone, I'm going to bed'.

Really, the dialogue in books is a *stylised* version of the way people speak. It's neatened and edited and air-brushed and colour-filtered. It has to create the illusion of intimacy or professionalism or madness in a much shorter word count and much tidier sentences than you'd actually find in real life. As writers, we have to edit out, 'So, how was your day?' and 'Oh, yeah, no, if you could, no, doesn't matter, I was just, never mind', and cut quickly to 'Why the hell didn't you tell me about the baby?'

Lilian Darcy

15

THICKENING YOUR
plot and conflict

THE EMOTIONAL JOURNEY

From a personal perspective, I prefer to plot. I like to have a loose plan of what I want to happen, my characters to achieve, some stumbling blocks, and—characteristic of the Presents/Modern/Sexy line—the emotional journey my characters will take. I note down some ideas, begin fleshing them out, decide which ideas definitely fit, and put aside the possibles. By now I've usually developed a technicolour filmstrip of the story in my head—given everyday life and numerous family distractions, I've learned not to trust my memory.

I make notes! Lots of notes. (The trick is to have a pad, notepad, whatever, and use the same one! Or have a clipboard and attach all the scraps of paper to it.) I like to write in scenes—I know it doesn't work for some—and then link the scenes together. If everything is going well, I can usually manage a scene in a day or two, so there's an ongoing sense of achievement. And it sure as hell beats the middle-book slump where, if you're writing from beginning to end, the story tends to sag and there's a lot of extraneous detail which doesn't move the story forward.

Helen Bianchin

NEW PLOT TWISTS

Many editors say the plot in a romance novel is a given— the hero and heroine meet and are powerfully attracted; something gets in the way of their attraction (conflict) and solving the 'something' leads to the happy ending. Since the conflict has to last for anything from 50 000 to 100 000 or more words, it needs to be something stronger than mutual dislike, or a misunderstanding capable of being resolved if the characters simply talk to each other.

Hard though it is to believe now, a marriage of convenience (when the characters agree to marry for reasons other than love) was a new plot idea once. Likewise, some of the other perennials of the genre— one of the characters having amnesia, twins switching places, the 'secret baby' the hero doesn't know he's fathered—all remain popular with romance readers, although these days, it pays to give the conventional plot your own fresh twist. What if the heroine is pretending to have amnesia so she can investigate the hero's business dealings without arousing his suspicion? Or the twins haven't changed places at all, but the hero only thinks they have? This kind of thinking is not only fun, it gives rise to some wonderful new twists on reader favourites.

Valerie Parv

GOAL, MOTIVATION, CONFLICT

This is an area where I freeze like a rabbit in car headlights if I have to think about it on too technical a level. I would sooner clean mouldy bathroom tile grouting with a toothbrush for six hours straight than attend a one-hour workshop on 'Goal, Motivation and Conflict'.

I really panic about it. Plot? Conflict? I feel disorganised and inadequate for not having those things neatly laid out on a chart, and for not even being able to respond in a more stream-of-consciousness way to the question, 'What is the book about?'

But that's just me. And I wouldn't necessarily recommend it as the best approach. I would sincerely like to be efficiently on top of plot, conflict and story, but my process seems to involve feeling around in the dark until I grab hold of something, pull it out into the light, and decide on closer examination that there's a possibility it might fit as a life-changing moment or significant past event or unsolved emotional issue for the fairly complex character I've drawn in my head.

My advice to other writers would be: if you do have a sizzling sense of plot, story and conflict from very early in the piece, go for it. That's your process and your strength. Celebrate it and make it even stronger if you can. If you don't, however, then you're not alone, and it doesn't mean you can't pull together all the complicated strands necessary to create a book. It does probably mean you'll take longer, or throw more pages away, or agonise more. But you'll get there in the end.

Lilian Darcy

DIGGING DEEPER

I plot madly. I weave all sorts of webs, write character profiles and know *exactly* where my story is going . . . and then I start writing. At that point my main characters come to life, often quite differently to how I intended. So I have to re-plot and throw out the profiles. And then other characters appear, secondary characters who push the plot in different directions again. (I've tried to circumvent this by doing even more plotting and character profiles before I start writing. Doesn't work for me.) The secret is to be flexible. Be prepared to alter direction just as you would if life threw you a curve ball. Be prepared to dig deeper into your characters and the stuff of your story. Chances are it will be an improvement on your original idea.

People like to ask writers: 'Where do you get your ideas?' To be honest, the initial idea is only a very tiny part of the whole process. Anyone can have an idea, and by itself an idea is useless. You have to work with it, flesh it out, play around and maybe do some research to check that it's going to work. And even then, when you start writing and the characters come to life, you have to be prepared for your original, beautiful idea to start looking very different. I used to panic about that and try to stick to the original premise. Wasn't that being professional and self-disciplined? What it was being was stupid and ignoring what Barbara Samuel on her website, barbarasamuel.com, calls 'the girls in the basement'. Listen to your girls and refine and polish your ideas. Never be afraid to change your mind. The original premise of your story is not sacred. If it wants to turn into something better, help it.

Elizabeth Rolls

GROWING YOUR THEME

All good writing must be about something. The something is the idea that prompts you to start writing in the first place. This doesn't mean preaching or writing what publishers call 'issues books' disguised as fiction. By all means explore issues in journalistic form, but in your fiction, allow your characters to express their own points of view. As the saying goes in Hollywood, 'If you've got a message, send it Western Union'.

As the author, you may still develop a theme, but generally it won't be identifiable until after you've written the book. Suddenly you'll see that you've written a novel exploring the effects of divorce on members of a family, or you've highlighted the problems dislocation causes for children.

It's better if you don't try to define your theme at the start. Instead, aim to create interesting, believable characters with real problems and conflicts, and the theme will grow of its own accord, becoming all the more effective when 'shown' through the characters, rather than being 'told' by the author.

Valerie Parv

'LEAPFROGGING'

I really wish I could plot every move out to the tiniest detail before I start writing but, unfortunately, that's not how my brain works. I usually have an opening scene and, more often than not, the ending in my head. Then I do detailed character charts and get to know my characters. I'll jot down scenes and ideas as they come to me and plot out the first few chapters before I start writing. Then I plot the next few chapters using the plot points I have written down. So I guess I'm a combination of pantser and plotter, although I have heard this method of plotting a few chapters and writing them before plotting the next few referred to as 'leapfrogging'.

If you're writing an erotic romance novella as opposed to a full-length novel, you have to approach the plotting from a different angle. You have a very short page count in which to get your characters to not only fall in love, but also to fall into bed. Because your plot has to be tight and you have to move things along quickly, it often pays to give your characters some prior romantic history. As for conflict, construct it around sex and you won't have any problems getting your characters to jump into bed.

Alexis Fleming

KEEP YOUR STORY BREATHING

It takes very little to spark off a story idea, but it takes a wealth of effort and brainpower to keep your idea and story breathing. Normally a title or a character's name will pop into my head and I build a story around it. Sometimes I fill out a character chart listing the ins and outs of my characters. Then I come up with a word-count goal, and work out how many chapters I'll need. I also work out what my starting point, middle goal and end goal will be. In between, I'm a pantser and let the characters dictate the story. If I get too far ahead of myself, my characters pull me back into line.

If I get hung up then I plot a more intricate outline for that chapter. Conflict and tension move the story along, so I try to add in both internal and external conflict. Internal = emotional; external = accident, danger, misunderstanding, etc. My characters will always tell me if they agree or not. They're the boss.

Kelly Ethan

RESEARCH MORE THAN FACTS

People have a strange definition of what research is. Sure, it's about facts, but it's also about smells and textures and sounds and tastes. What does an operating theatre smell like? What sounds are made during surgery? How do doctors, or eighteenth-century courtesans, 'feel'? That's why you can't just get research from books. Or if you have to just get it from books, you have to do an enormous amount of work with your imagination to bring those facts off the page and translate them into senses and feelings. I've set books, both Medical Romances and Silhouettes, in places I haven't been, and you have to look at photos and feel yourself into them. You're hunting for clues in every detail. There are big rocks in that picture, sitting in the sunshine. Do they feel hot to the heroine's touch? Do they appear a different colour in the early-morning light?

People say 'write what you know'. I say 'you know more than you think'. And also, if you stick purely to what you know, even if you've had a varied and interesting life, you'll run out of situations after a few books. You *must* do research.

Lilian Darcy

PLOTTING GUIDE

The wedding maxim 'something old, something new, something borrowed, something blue' is a good guide to plotting your novel. *Something old* can be the bones of the story, so timeless they can be mistaken for a formula. Basically, you have two people who are instantly, powerfully attracted, but face an obstacle to their love. The story's appeal lies as much in who these two people are, and how they resolve their differences, as in what happens along the way.

Something borrowed refers to the traditions of romance going all the way back to Jane Austen. Romances provide a welcome escape from reality, so shouldn't be sordid or depressing, although you can deal with real issues. Myths such as Cinderella and Beauty and the Beast are often retold in contemporary romance.

Something blue is the obstacle or conflict keeping the lovers apart. The conflict you choose should be strong enough to last the whole book through, rather than a simple misunderstanding.

Something new is the element which makes your story one of the ten in 5000 manuscripts submitted to romance editors which are accepted. Publishers say they want fresh, original stories rather than clones of existing books. Original doesn't mean bizarre or exotic, but rather your own unique way of telling the story.

Valerie Parv

ONE MAJOR PROBLEM

If you want to write a very intense romance, be sure your central tension or conflict is strong enough to engender deep emotion. Important secrets, shattering betrayals, grave injustices, ruthless revenge, serious clashes of values and beliefs rather than mere differences of opinion. Things that can alter lives and characters make the most involving, page-turning plots. A series of small misunderstandings (although they may usefully complicate a plot) does not have half the impact of one really major problem, one formidable and seemingly insurmountable stumbling block to happiness, around which the entire plot and story are built.

Daphne Clair

FROM 'WHAT IF?' TO 'WHY?'

As writers we all revere the question 'what if?' for it is there our fantasies begin, but an even more important question for me is, 'why?', and I ask it all the time as I write. Why is my hero behaving so objectionably? Why is my heroine so afraid of love? It's all about motivation, and the most far-fetched plot can be believable if you can provide credible reasons for your characters to be acting the way they are.

Take, for example, a heroine who has grown up in a poor area of a big city, her family ground down by poverty, her life a struggle to get ahead. Through brains and hard work and sheer tenacity she becomes a doctor. Now, it would be feasible for her to never want to see that neighbourhood again, to be determined never to be poor again, or it could go the other way, and it would be equally believable that she might want to go back and work there because it's so hard to get doctors in that area and she wants to help.

Force the woman to return to her origins—sent back

there by the hero boss, maybe—and you have conflict: internal conflict from the guilt she feels because she hates being there, and external conflict with the hero putting her in this position.

Alternatively, you can take the second heroine, who *wants* to go back because of the doctor shortage, and set up a scenario where she needs money to start a clinic to help the people with whom she grew up. So she agrees to work in a high-society health farm where the pay is excellent, but she feels the work is less rewarding. She would learn that the wealthy people are as vulnerable as the poor she knows so well, and in all likelihood, they'd end up funding the clinic, while the hero turns out not to be the money-hungry sod she first labelled him. Both scenarios would work, but the first would be the most powerful.

To me, motivation is the most useful weapon in the writer's armoury, for it can take your story anywhere you want it to go, adding tension, anxiety and stress, and helping to build your conflict into a surging force.

Meredith Webber

16

MARKETING
your book

WHY WRITE A SYNOPSIS?

I don't know any writer, me included, who likes writing a synopsis. Yet today the majority of editors ask to see a synopsis before they will look at a complete manuscript, so there's no avoiding the pain. I find it helps to imagine that I'm writing the copy for the jacket of the book. If a reader comes across the book in a bookstore, what would make them want to buy the book?

The main difference between a synopsis and a book jacket is that in the synopsis, you need to explain how the story ends. No editor wants to be told they should read the book to find out what happens. They want to see your writing style, and whether or not you can bring the story to a successful conclusion.

Valerie Parv

FIND COMMON GROUND

As writers, it's our job to find the common ground, the big and small things which can appeal to a wide range of readers, and use those things to create globally appealing stories with themes that resonate with a maximum number of people.

From the publisher's perspective, it makes good business sense to want as many readers as possible. From the writer's perspective, I think we write because there's a part of us that wants to connect to our readers, to feel as if our stories are their stories, that they matter to us, so we're looking for that union and intersection as well.

Jennie Adams

PITCHING YOUR BOOK

The latest way to sell your book is through the *pitch*, the chance to give a verbal sales pitch for your book to an agent or editor at a writers' conference. Pitching appointments are usually short, only five to ten minutes on average, giving you very little time to get the editor enthused about your work. You need to polish and rehearse your pitch ahead of time. Break your plot down to the essentials of what happens (plot), who it happens to (hero and heroine), and conflict. You can also add a sentence or two about the main crisis between your hero and heroine, and how it helps them to resolve their differences.

Editors also like you to mention any story 'hooks' your book contains. A hook is romance industry shorthand for any of the classic romance themes such as single dads, amnesia, twins, marriages of convenience, royalty, cowboys, small-town setting, military, Beauty and the Beast, and Cinderella. Try to explain how your use of the chosen hook is unique.

Being able to break your book down to a paragraph of essential information is good practice for writing query letters and later for handling media interviews (thinking positive here) after your book is published.

Valerie Parv

GETTING UNSTUCK

If you don't fall in love with the book you're writing, it won't work, and yet sometimes the magic doesn't happen on its own. We've sent off a sketchy idea and, shock-horror, the editor wants to see a partial and we're not creatively ready. Or the character looked good on paper but just doesn't gel when we start to write. Or maybe we're contracted to do a sequel or spin-off and are locked into a certain story-line. If we do the right work to find and explore the meaning and importance of what we're writing, whether it's in the broad themes, the central characters or the tiny details, then we can get beyond the feeling of being stuck and uninspired, and find the love.

Lilian Darcy

MARKET RESEARCH

Take the time to research your market. Know which publisher is publishing the sort of book you are writing. If possible, find out which editor is buying them. Find out what their submission procedure is. Give them what they want. If they want a brief query letter and a two-page synopsis, then don't send the story of your life and a ten-page synopsis. For the letter, stick to the relevant facts; mention any prior publications, writing experience, contest wins. Keep everything professional. For the synopsis, don't wander off into extraneous detail. Stay focused on the important elements of your story. Do not leave out the resolution in an attempt to make the editor request the whole manuscript just to find out! You have to show him/her that you can make the whole thing work. Cheap tricks are off the menu.

Elizabeth Rolls

SELF-PROMOTION

To date, all of my sales have been through digital publishers. Although some of my novels have now gone to print as well, I can only talk promotion and marketing as it pertains to the e-book market. I write for the American and the United Kingdom markets so I have to rely on the internet to get my promotional message across. The most important tool is a good website, updated frequently. Nothing is worse than going to an author's website and finding there have been no changes for the last six months. I actually employ a marketing company in the United States which not only updates my website monthly, but also sends out press releases, monthly newsletters, etc. and generally keeps me on track with where I should be spending my promo dollar. I have a Yahoo group that I try to interact with on a regular basis. These ladies are fantastic and talk my books up all over the internet. Whenever I have a new release, I have cover or banner ads up at all the major review sites, such as The Romance Studio, Romance Junkies, Coffee Time Romance and many more. I take part in online chats wherever possible and generally make a major effort to get my name out there among the readers.

When it comes to my print books, I advertise each new release in *Romance Sells*, a catalogue produced by Romance Writers of America, and sent out to

American booksellers and libraries. I also combine with other authors to have a full page advertisement in *Romantic Times*. I've made some good contacts at conferences and I regularly send promo items to bookstores in the United States. It's all about keeping your name out there.

Alexis Fleming

IMPROVE YOUR CHANCES

There are three ways you can improve your chances of success. One is to make sure your story is a romance. It should not be, say, a spy story in which two people happen to fall in love. All the events in the book must contribute to how the hero and heroine feel about each other, either bringing them closer together, or pushing them further apart until the reader doubts they can ever overcome their differences and reach their happy ending. If the heroine discovers the hero has lied to her, how does she feel? Does it confirm her worst fears? Or has she started to trust him and now feels betrayed? Answering these questions results in a page-turning story which involves the reader.

The second way is to keep your hero and heroine together as much as possible, even under the same roof if you can make it work. This not only keeps the focus on the main relationship, it saves you having to contrive ways to get them together.

Finally, your story must pack an emotional punch. Romance editors frequently report receiving manuscripts where there is a lot happening, but little in the way of emotional tension which encourages the reader to read on. One editor advises letting yourself go and writing your own emotional experiences into your characters.

Valerie Parv

BUILD ON PLOT POINTS

The dreaded synopsis! When I first started writing, I did the synopsis after I'd written the story. Now my books are accepted on proposal (synopsis and sample chapters), I've taught myself to do the synopsis first. If you're like me and write by the seat of your pants, that can be difficult. I tend to take each of my plot points and build a paragraph around each one until I've fleshed it out enough so that an editor can see at a glance what the story is about. At least I'm learning to plot a bit more before I start writing, and I must admit that makes the writing go faster.

Alexis Fleming

A 'GOOD' REJECTION

Only in the writing world is a failure described as a 'good' rejection. Yes, there really is such a thing.

A good rejection is one where an editor takes the time to comment on your manuscript and make specific suggestions for how to improve it. Curiously, the longer the rejection letter you receive, the closer you are to acceptance. Editors are too busy to spend time encouraging a writer who has no chance of succeeding, so they generally only offer substantial help and encouragement to those they feel might have 'the write stuff'.

It's also true that rejections come back more quickly then good news, mainly because a manuscript with potential passes through many hands, progressing upward through the editorial chain of command until a decision is made to buy the book.

Valerie Parv

HOOKING AN EDITOR

At this point we're talking marketing to an editor, not to chain bookstore accounts or the reading public, but of course editors have their eye on the likely reactions of exactly those people. The sad fact is that we're all impatient now. We want to be hooked immediately. We don't want to waste time trying to work out what the story is about, or what sort of feel it has—we want instant information, and if you can give this to an editor upfront in your synopsis and query letter then she's going to read what follows with greater attention.

If you have an obvious hook or a really striking premise that you can capture in a couple of pithy phrases, don't bury those things on page seven of your synopsis, put them in right at the beginning. If you can't find your brilliant hook or premise, maybe someone else can. Sometimes we're too close to our own work—if we could summarise it in a couple of sentences, we wouldn't have to write the book. If you have a critique partner, friend or relative that you trust, or if you're lucky enough to be working with a mentor or teacher, see if they can cut to the heart of what your book is about and give you some ideas.

I like to brainstorm this kind of thing, the way I might brainstorm a whole scene, or title ideas. Give yourself permission to write down lists of scattered words, phrases and ideas in no logical order, without having to create perfect sentences or justify what you're putting down. Sometimes you can surprise yourself with what comes out, and later on you can put it together in the right way. At this point, you're throwing out your net and catching as many different fish as you can. Eventually, you'll sort them out and throw the bad ones back into the sea.

Almost every writer I know hates to write synopses and query letters, and some of us are lucky enough to get to the point where we don't have to do it anymore.

We have a good relationship with our editor, and she trusts that when we write 'and then stuff happens' in the middle of a story outline, we're actually going to come up with some good scenes. Until this blissful period in our career arrives, however, we're stuck with synopsis writing and we just have to grit out teeth and do it, recognising that for some of us it will take more drafts and more polishing than the actual book. At least it's shorter!

Lilian Darcy

AGENT SECRETS

I'm often asked if you need an agent to get a book accepted. Initially, I sold many books without an agent. But having been represented by Linda Tate of The Tate Gallery since 1993, I can say that she smoothes my career path considerably. While an agent can't sell a bad book, they free your time to write the best books you can. These days they also do much of the reading that was allocated to publishers' readers, and many editors now only look at books sent via an agent. Harlequin is one of the few publishers still accepting submissions from authors directly. One way for a new writer to gain representation is to market your book yourself initially, then invite an agent to take over once an editor shows interest.

Valerie Parv

17

THE WRITING *life*

FEED YOUR MUSE

You have to feed your muse; don't forget that she needs as much attention as a child or a pet. Or a spouse/lover/partner. So read. Then read some more. Find out which stories you love. Travel. Write. Watch movies. Write. Read books on writing, like Robert McKee's *Story: Substance, Structure, Style and the Principles of Screenwriting* (Methuen, 1999), or Stephen King's *On Writing: A Memoir of the Craft* (Pocket, 2002). Relate what they say to your own writing. Take long walks if you get stuck, and your muse seems to have gone AWOL. Scribble down the ideas that come to you and play with them. Travel again if you've paid off the credit card.

Elizabeth Rolls

WRITE EVERY DAY

If being a published author is your goal, then you have to work at it. You have to keep at it and you have to be disciplined. Write every day, even if it's something you'll delete on the following day. Keep writing, regardless of the rejections that may come your way.

Alexis Fleming

PLUNGE IN AND WRITE

Trying to write the perfect book is a good way to get nothing done. What if it only turns out so-so? Are you the best judge? At different times, two students at my workshops said they thought the only books worth writing were bestsellers. They saw no point in writing 'just another book'.

They overlooked that history makes these judgements, not the writers. The best we could do is to analyse a large number of bestselling books and identify common denominators. Using this approach, Hollywood has produced some astonishingly expensive flops.

If life is indeed what happens to you while you're busy making other plans, then a bestseller is what happens to an ordinary book when the author pours her heart and soul into it and her passion communicates itself to millions of readers.

If you put off writing because you fear your work won't be good enough, the only solution is to plunge in and write. Abandon the belief that your work must be perfect on the first, or even the fiftieth, draft. Concentrate on the story you desperately want to tell. Let your passion and commitment carry you away, and there's a good chance they'll have the same effect on your readers.

Valerie Parv

FIND COMMON GROUND

We joke that writing is as simple as puncturing a vein and letting the blood pour onto the page. And sometimes it is about exposure, letting readers into the heart and soul of you. The more you dip into your own emotions, heart, world outlook, feelings about life, religion, the universe, the possibility of life on other planets, anything that matters to you, the more you'll find common ground with your readers, who are also seeking answers to the age-old questions of love and life and how it all fits together, or falls apart and manages to be rebuilt.

Jennie Adams

IDEAL vs REALITY

Ah, there's the ideal writing day . . . and the reality. On an ideal day, I'd edit and rewrite the previous day's work in the morning, then write a minimum of five pages in the afternoon. The reality is that some days the words flow like gold, and other days every word is like pulling teeth . . . painful. I aim for twenty good, edited and rewritten pages a week.

Helen Bianchin

ESCAPISM

The best thing about writing romance is knowing the pleasure I'm giving to readers. I think about my books giving much-needed time-out to thousands of women around the world and that's a worthwhile thing to do. It really makes me angry that predominantly male forms of escapism, like watching football on TV, are accorded such serious attention and respect, while our predominantly female form of escapism, romance fiction, which offers very similar benefits, is ridiculed or ignored. Please don't ever put me in the same room with someone who has no need for escapism in their life. They're not human.

Lilian Darcy

SETTING DEADLINES

For books without deadlines, I set my own and they become as fixed as any set by an editor. Two hints about setting your own deadlines: set them just beyond your personal comfort zone so you'll work just that bit harder. This ensures you have some extra time up your sleeve to deal with unanticipated problems without missing your deadline.

Do not include the extra month in the deadline you've set for yourself. For you, the extra time doesn't exist. Giving others your real deadline leaves you no scope to be appreciated as a miracle worker. Hence the double deadline: the private one for yourself, and the one you agree to in the contract with your publisher. With practice, you'll become skilled at estimating and setting your own deadlines until they're as pressing to you as those in any contract.

Valerie Parv

LEARN FROM OTHERS

My greatest advice for a beginning writer is to join a writing or critique group. It's amazing how much you can learn from others. A good critique group is worth its weight in gold. Read, read, read in the genre you want to focus your writing on. Then sit down at your computer and write. It doesn't matter how bad you think it is, write it anyway. Develop the habit of writing every day. As bestselling author Nora Roberts said when she appeared at a Romance Writers of Australia conference a few years ago: 'You can edit a bad page, but you can't edit a blank page.' How true! And most importantly, don't ever give up your dream.

Alexis Fleming

PATIENCE AND PERSEVERANCE

For me, reading and writing equals breathing. Without either, I would be an insane gibbering mess. The best attributes someone can bring to writing are patience, determination and perseverance. If a book isn't flowing, you need to keep pushing on. Be determined no matter the hurdles or distractions. Take said hurdles and turn them into motivation or even plot ideas, but keep going. If you need to, unplug your phone and internet. No matter what, keep writing and, most importantly, enjoy what you do.

Kelly Ethan

KEEP A WRITING DIARY

'The unexamined life is not worth living', wrote Socrates. I'd argue that it's equally important to lead a well-examined writing life. As writers, most of us are too prone to anxiety and self-doubt over our natural talent, our understanding of the market, the state of our career . . . Basically, anything we *can* worry about, we *will*. If we can convert some of this amorphous, billowing angst into productive assessment and self-examination, we can save ourselves a lot of stress as well as streamlining our process and honing our skills.

I recommend keeping some kind of writing diary. I'm not a big proponent of rigid rules with regard to writing timetables and disciplines. For me the overarching rule is always 'Do what works', so I'd never say to anyone, 'You have to write in your diary every day'. Instead, I'd advise making a writing diary into whatever you want and need it to be—highly structured and disciplined, filled with scrapbook items and photos, a long stream of consciousness about whatever is on your mind, anything.

Mine is a complete mess. I use it to vent about career doubts and frustrations, jot down story ideas, structure doomed attempts at coherent timetables, scribble everything from character notes to shopping lists. Sometimes I'll write in it every day for a couple of weeks, then more than a month might go by without an entry.

One of its big values for me is the way it can teach me about myself as a writer through the hindsight of reading back through past entries. Turns out I *always* have those few days of crashing doubt about three-quarters of the way through a book. And that maddening sense of progress grinding to a halt? That's a signal from my wise and creative subconscious mind that I've gone off track earlier in the story and need to go back and make some changes.

Maintaining a long writing career is not easy. It can be lonely and discouraging, it demands a huge commitment to keeping ourselves creatively fresh, there's very little job security except for those at the very top of the bestseller lists, and there are far too many ways in which we can compare ourselves to others in our field and conclude that we come up short.

I believe that it's crucial to pay attention to self-nourishment and am constantly on the lookout for new ways to do it. We need to take care of our physical health, and pay close attention to the idea of balance in our lives. Since writing is solitary, we need to find ways to interact with people. Since writing involves an output of energy—and don't underestimate how physically, mentally and emotionally draining a writing day can be, even a successful and uplifting one—we need to find ways to put that energy back in. Since writing is sedentary, we need to find ways to get our bodies moving. Since writing can involve long droughts between positive feedback or signposts of success, we need to learn to reward ourselves in the meantime.

I'm going to return to Socrates and stress once again that you should examine your writing life, and don't ever take it for granted.

Lilian Darcy

SIT DOWN AND WRITE

The most important advice I ever read, and the advice I pass on to all would-be writers, is sit down and write. Thinking about doing it, talking about doing it, going to lectures and conferences, and joining professional associations are all important, but nothing is as important as actually sitting down and writing. As a newbie writer I was fortunate enough to meet the incomparable Helen Bianchin and she told me about the writing muscle in the brain that had to be exercised like any other muscle. So exercise it: sit down and write—write every day if you can, even if it's only for a few minutes. Describe a scene that catches your eye, jot down a phrase you read or hear that sounds good. As a writer you are also a collector—a collector of words and phrases, of images and emotions. Listen, watch, feel and write. Easy, isn't it?

Meredith Webber

HEARTENING READS

My theory is that, of all my books, my romance novels would be the ones most likely to survive a global catastrophe. As a reader hurrying to shelter as disaster looms, I don't think I'd be likely to pick up an encyclopaedia to read in the uncertain hours ahead. Instead, I'd grab the most heartening book to hand: the romance I was currently reading. And like the artefacts from Pompeii, the humble love story is what would rise phoenix-like from the ashes. It's a reassuring notion.

Valerie Parv

Index